Workplace transport safety

An employers' guide

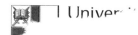

D0496477

HSE Books

This guidance is issued by the Health and Safety Executive.
Following the guidance is not compulsory and you are free
to take other action. But if you do follow the guidance you
will normally be doing enough to comply with the law. Health
and safety inspectors seek to secure compliance with the
law and may refer to this guidance as illustrating good
practice.

Contents

Introduction

About this guide

Who is this guide for?

1   This guidance has been written for employers, including managers and supervisors. It may also be useful for safety and union representatives, contractors, the self-employed and employees.

What is this guide for?

2   Every year, about 50 people are killed in accidents involving workplace transport.

3   These types of accidents also cause more than 1500 major injuries (accidents which, for example, result in broken bones or amputations) and about 3500 injuries that cause people to be off work for more than three days.

4   We (the Health and Safety Executive) have published this guide to help employers, managers and supervisors make accidents involving workplace transport less likely. It will also be useful for safety representatives, self-employed people, contractors, vehicle operators, other employees, trade associations, commercial landlords and other organisations concerned with workplace transport safety.

5   The guide is split into the following sections:

■   The *Introduction* provides some background to workplace transport safety, and to health and safety in general in Great Britain.

■   *Guidance for managers* gives advice to people responsible for a workplace on how they can make sure that workplace transport is safe. It includes guidance about:
-    assessing risks;
-    organisational measures; and
-    how to make sure the site, drivers and vehicles are all organised for safety.

■   *Operational guidance* gives advice about:
-    common vehicle operations;
-    some risks that are often associated with them; and
-    how you could deal with safety for each type of operation.

6   It is likely that some of these sections will be more relevant for you than other sections, so you can use this guidance as the foundation for your risk assessment in these areas.

Figure 1 An HGV parking area

7   You can read this guide as a whole, or you can go straight to relevant sections, which can be read on their own.

8   It will never be possible to create a guide that covers every risk. Your workplace will have risks that are specific to your location, your type of work, the people you employ, the vehicles you use and the way you do things. Use the *Managing the risks* and *Operational guidance* sections to give yourself an idea of the sort of things you should consider when you think about vehicle safety in the workplace.

9   This information is suitable for medium and large industrial and commercial sites, but should also be useful for smaller businesses and for places such as construction sites, quarries, farms and forestry operations. Guidance documents specifically relating to these industries are also available, which you should refer to if you work in these industries.

10   You do not have to follow this guidance. However, if you do follow it, you will normally be doing enough to comply with the law.

11   Health and safety inspectors work to make sure people follow the law and may use this guidance to show examples of good practice.

12   We do not accept responsibility for any action or decision you take based on interpreting this guidance. If you are in any doubt, you should consult someone who is competent in workplace transport issues.

The benefits for business

13   The cost of managing good health and safety is normally quite visible, but the cost of failing to control risks is often absorbed into other operating costs and so is harder to see.

14   As well as personal distress, a relatively minor accident (for example, one which results in a few days off work) is likely to cost around £3500. A major accident can cost around £30 000 – a cost which the employer normally has to pay.

15   Costs of an accident to a business can include:

■   repairing or replacing damaged capital;
■   loss of or damage to goods;
■   insurance costs;
■   compensation payments;
■   legal costs;
■   paying for the time that people aren't working because of the accident – such as paying the injured person, anyone helping them, people cleaning up, investigations;
■   less efficient replacement workers, and the cost of training them;
■   lost production efficiency;
■   damaged reputation;
■   damaged employee morale; and
■   resulting costs to customers, especially where 'just-in-time' logistics processes are used.

16   Businesses that effectively manage workplace transport risks benefit from:

■   reduced loss through damage, injury and people off work;
■   better insurance rates;
■   avoiding compensation payments, fines and legal costs;
■   a protected reputation;
■   improved employee morale; and
■   the general improvements in working practices that result from a planned and sensible approach to safety, which can lead to improvements in productivity.

17   Apart from the moral and legal reasons for protecting people's health, safety and welfare, accidents are financially bad for business. See our guide *Reduce risks – cut costs*[1] for more information on the costs of accidents at work.

What is 'workplace transport'?

18   'Workplace transport' means any vehicle or piece of mobile equipment that is used by employers, employees, self-employed people or visitors in any work setting (apart from travelling on public roads).

19   It covers a very wide range of vehicles, from cars, vans, lorries and lift trucks, to less common vehicles and plant such as straddle carriers, rubber-tyred gantries and self-propelled machinery.

20   The word 'vehicle' in this guidance refers to all of the different vehicles found at the workplace, including mobile equipment.

21   Vehicles moving on public roads are not usually classed as 'workplace transport', even though they may carry people who are working, such as haulage drivers. This is because road traffic laws cover traffic risks on public roads in more detail than general health and safety law.

22   However, public roads are often used as temporary workplaces, for example:

■   during roadworks or roadside deliveries;
■   for breakdown assistance; or
■   for other roadside work.

23   See *Public roads as workplaces* (paragraphs 234-237) for more information about health and safety for people working on or next to public roads. For advice about work-related road safety, you should read our free leaflet *Driving at work*.[2]

24   This guide does not deal with safety for air, water, rail or specialised underground mining transport, although it may be relevant for general vehicles used in these industries.

Types of accident

25   Most transport accidents involve moving vehicles (including people being hit or run over), people falling from vehicles, people being hit by falling objects (usually part of the load) or vehicles overturning.

26   Vehicles are particularly dangerous when they are reversing, because it can be difficult for drivers to see what is going on behind them.

27   However, the root causes of accidents are usually due to poor management control.

28   Managers often fail to provide a safe site, safe vehicles or safe systems of work, or fail to make sure that safe systems are followed (usually through too little information, instruction, training or supervision).

29   Most transport accidents can be prevented if managers:

■   carry out a thorough risk assessment;
■   set and monitor safe ways of working with vehicles; and
■   raise people's awareness of the risks involved.

Safe sites, vehicles and drivers
30   Accidents involving workplace transport are often caused by failures in several different areas. When you assess how well workplace transport risks are being controlled, you should look at the following three areas in particular.

Safe site
31   Check to see whether the site has well-defined traffic routes that are free from obstructions, and that have firm and even surfaces. Check to see that:

■   every effort has been made to separate pedestrians from vehicles ('segregation');
■   there are safe crossing places for pedestrians to get across vehicle routes; and
■   there is an effective one-way system – especially for large goods vehicles.

Safe vehicles
32   Check that there is an effective maintenance programme for steering and braking systems, and for vehicle lights. Check that reversing aids, 'roll-over protection systems' and driver restraints have been fitted where they are appropriate. You can find much more information about these things in the chapter *Safe vehicles* and in the section *Operational guidance*.

Safe drivers
33   Check that drivers' behaviour is supervised and that drivers are trained and competent. In particular, you should be able to provide evidence (for example, to a health and safety inspector) that people using lift trucks have been trained to the standards described in *Driver training and competence* (paragraphs 642-665) in the chapter *Safe drivers*.

34   You must manage all three of these areas well for workplace transport risks to be controlled effectively. This book reflects these three areas, to help you make sensible decisions that will make your workplace safer.

Important note: 'reasonably practicable'

35   The phrase 'reasonably practicable' is very important for health and safety in Great Britain. It is used to decide how much action should be taken to keep risks under control at work.

36   Sensible health and safety is about managing risks – risks can rarely be eliminated altogether. The phrase 'reasonably practicable' is a legal phrase used to help you decide what you have to do manage risks sensibly.

37   The law says that every business in Great Britain has to:

■   be aware of risks to health and safety in the workplace; and
■   take 'reasonably practicable' steps to control these risks, and to make accidents less likely.

38   For a step to be 'reasonably practicable', the cost must be sensible compared to the benefit (reasonable), and it must be physically possible in the first place (practicable).

39   The cost is the money, time or trouble involved in putting a safety measure in place and maintaining it.

40   The benefit is the smaller chance of anyone being harmed. This is usually achieved by making the possibility of an accident happening an 'insignificant risk'; or perhaps by making it less likely that someone will be seriously hurt if an accident does happen.

41   If the cost is sensible compared to the benefit, a measure is probably 'reasonably practicable'. For example, sweeping the load bed of a lorry to help make sure loads don't slide around on the dusty surface should be quite cheap, and the benefit is very worthwhile, so it is likely to be 'reasonably practicable'.

42   If the cost is a lot higher than the benefit, it might not be 'reasonably practicable' to put the measure in place. In law, the words 'grossly disproportionate' are used to decide whether the cost is so high compared to the benefit that a measure is not 'reasonably practicable'.

43   Just because one measure might not be considered 'reasonably practicable' does not mean that there are not other, more appropriate measures that you can take.

44   You may want to take steps to control a risk that go further than the 'reasonably practicable' measures you must take by law. 'Reasonable practicability' is the lowest level of risk control that the law demands, not an upper limit.

45   It is important to know what 'reasonably practicable' does not mean:

■   it does not mean 'affordable'. You might be expected to do things that you would consider expensive, if the risk is serious enough to justify it. If the cost of a measure is not 'grossly disproportionate' to the benefit, the measure is 'reasonably practicable';

- it does not mean 'most expensive'. You are not expected to spend as much money as possible to control risks, if they can be controlled to the same level by cheaper methods.
- it does not mean 'common practice' or 'industry standard'. It makes no difference whether other people control similar risks in a similar way or a different way, or to a different level. Deciding what is 'reasonably practicable' is a judgement that has to be made for each risk individually;

46   **To keep the language as clear as possible, we have tried to explain the principle of 'reasonable practicability' clearly here, and have generally avoided using the phrase in the guidance itself.**

47   **Where this guidance advises action you should take to control risks, it means that you should take it, so far as it is 'reasonably practicable'. But the guidance also refers to specific legal requirements, some of which you must meet.**

48   This is only a very general explanation of what 'reasonably practicable' means. For a fuller explanation, please see *Redgrave's Health and Safety*[3] and our website at www.hse.gov.uk.[4]

49   Exactly what is considered 'reasonably practicable' will vary depending on the circumstances. However, if an accident happens, you may be asked to show to an inquest or a court that you took all reasonable steps to prevent that accident.

50   Ultimately, only the courts can provide an authoritative interpretation of the phrase 'reasonably practicable'.

Health and safety law

51   There are many specific legal duties relating to workplace transport, and some of them are quite complicated. Throughout this guide, we explain what you must do by law.

52   In this guide, we talk about legal duties with the phrases 'by law' and 'the law requires'. You will also find the words 'must', 'must not' and 'may', which show things that are or may be required by law.

53   There are also more general legal responsibilities which apply to all situations.

54   Employers must:

- take all 'reasonably practicable' precautions to ensure the health, safety and welfare of all workers in the workplace and members of the public who might be affected by their activities;
- assess the risks to the health and safety of anyone affected by what they do (including employees and members of the public). If the company consists of five or more people, the significant findings must be recorded. See the chapter *Managing the risks* for more information;

- use certain 'principles of prevention' (which we describe in paragraph 60), where they take 'preventive measures' to control risks;
- effectively plan, organise, control, monitor and review the preventive and protective measures they use. If the company consists of five or more people, these arrangements must be recorded;
- so far as is 'reasonably practicable', provide and maintain safe systems of work;
- provide information, instruction, training and supervision to protect, so far as is 'reasonably practicable', employees' health and safety at work;
- maintain in a 'safe condition' (without risks to health) any workplace under their control, and the means of 'access' to and 'egress' from it (the way employees get into and out of the workplace).

55   If you are self-employed, you have a similar duty to that of employers – you must reduce as far as is 'reasonably practicable' risks to your own and other people's health and safety.

56   Anyone in control of work premises (for example, a landlord) has limited legal duties to make sure that the premises are safe. This also applies to people in control of the means of entering or leaving a workplace (for example, land that has to be crossed).

57   The phrase 'reasonably practicable' is very important, and we explain it more fully in paragraphs 35-50.

58   All employees must take reasonable care of their own and others' health and safety and co-operate with their employer so that the employer can meet their duties. Employees need to recognise this responsibility and act accordingly.

59   If you or your employees fail to meet the duties above, you or they might be prosecuted.

60   The 'principles of prevention' are set out in law. You must use them when you are putting in place measures to control risks. You need to try them in order, doing whatever is 'reasonably practicable' to reduce the risks. In summary, they are:

- avoiding risks;
- assessing the risks that cannot be avoided;
- tackling the source of the risks;
- adapting the work to the individual;
- adapting to technical progress;
- replacing anything dangerous with things that are less dangerous or not dangerous;
- developing a coherent overall prevention policy;
- giving joint protective measures priority over individual protective measures; and
- giving appropriate instructions to employees.

Phrases and meanings

61   We use the following phrases in this guidance (and elsewhere in health and safety) to mean quite specific things.

Competent person

62 A competent person is somebody who has enough knowledge, experience and personal ability, and who has received enough training and information, to do a task safely and well. The phrase 'competent person' is also used in some laws with a more specific meaning, which we explain in paragraph 614.

Duty holder

63 A duty holder is somebody who has a duty given to them by law. Every employer and worker is a duty holder in one way or another, because they have a duty to take reasonable care of themselves and other people. Employers, landlords and other people have other specific duties because of the nature of their relationship with people who are affected by what they do (for example, employees or tenants).

Hazard

64 A hazard means anything that can cause harm (for example, chemicals, electricity, working at height, machinery).

Risk

65 A risk is the chance that somebody will be harmed by the hazard (high or low) and how seriously they might be harmed (seriously or not). High risks are those where someone is very likely to be harmed or where the harm is likely to be serious (or both).

Risk assessment

66 A risk assessment is a careful look at what, in your work, could harm people. You should use your risk assessment to help you decide whether you have taken enough precautions or should do more to prevent harm.

Reasonably practicable

67 This is the level of action that the law says a person or business needs to take at work to reduce the chances of anyone being harmed. It means that everyone is expected to do everything they reasonably can to keep risks low. It is very important and we explain it in more detail in paragraphs 35-50.

System of work

68 A system of work is a way of doing a task. A safe system of work has to be identified for every aspect of work that an organisation does, to make sure that people are able to work safely. The system of work should be the result of a thorough risk assessment, which identifies what could harm people and how, so that these risks can be managed. The safe system should usually be written down so that workers can be instructed and their performance can be monitored.

Workplace

69 A workplace is any location where a person is working.

70 Public roads are public places and are covered by specific laws, so deciding when they are (or are not) workplaces can be complicated.

71 *What is 'workplace transport'?* (paragraphs 18-24) explains why public roads are usually not considered workplaces. See *Public roads as workplaces* (paragraphs 234-237) for more information about when public roads are used as temporary workplaces (for example, when they are sectioned off by road cones, or during a roadside delivery).

Guidance for managers

Managing the risks

72   By law, employers and self-employed people must assess the risks to anyone who might be affected by their work activity. These people should also take appropriate preventive and protective measures to control these risks.

73   These requirements apply to all work activities, including those involving transport (for example, driving, loading, sheeting, maintenance).

74   Our guide *Successful health and safety management*[5] identifies a three-stage plan you need to go through to manage risks – identifying hazards, assessing the risks and controlling the risks.

75   To help you carry out the plan, we recommend a risk assessment to cover all three stages at once.

Risk assessment

76   A risk assessment is nothing more than a careful examination of what, in your work, could harm people, so that you can weigh up whether you have done enough or should do more to prevent harm.

77   By law employers must assess risks as a way of finding out whether they are meeting legal duties. By law, the risk assessment must be 'suitable and sufficient'. Carrying out a risk assessment does not usually need to be very complicated or technical. Most employers carry out risk assessments during the normal course of their work. For example, when hiring new drivers, an employer would normally identify how much information, instruction or training they need, to make sure that they are able to carry out their duties without making mistakes or causing accidents. In recognising that there are risks associated with having new drivers, and then deciding what precautions to take, the employer has carried out a risk assessment and acted on it.

78   It is also important that your risk assessment is thorough and accurate because you need to use it when you decide what to do to control risks. It will help you to decide what is 'reasonably practicable' because it will help you decide how serious risks are, and how much effort and cost is necessary to control them. There is a section in this guide about what 'reasonably practicable' means – see paragraphs 35-50.

79   If your organisation employs five or more people (including managers), you must write down any significant findings from the risk assessment.

80   We recommend the following five-step process to carry out a risk assessment:

Step 1   Identify the hazards.

Step 2   Decide who might be harmed and how.

Step 3   Evaluate the risks and assess whether existing precautions are adequate.

Step 4   Record the significant findings.

Step 5   Review the risk assessment regularly, and as necessary.

81   There is an example of a risk-assessment form at the back of this guide (Appendix 2). You can fill this in as you work through the sections we explain below.

82   For more advice about doing a general risk assessment, you should read our free leaflet *Five steps to risk assessment*.[6] For more information about risk assessment in general, and laws with specific requirements for risk assessment, you should read our free guidance *A guide to risk assessment requirements*.[7]

Identifying the hazards

83   First you need to identify the work activities involving vehicles (including visiting vehicles) over a reasonable period. This could be over the course of a day, a week or maybe a month. You need to build up a clear picture of vehicle and pedestrian traffic in the workplace, and to make sure you miss nothing important.

84   Think through the activities you know happen, such as deliveries, loading activities or collecting waste. You can use the list in Table 1 to help you – just choose the activities that happen in your workplace, and add any others you can think of. You can do this by:

■   watching the workplace; and
■   paying attention to where vehicles are, what drivers are doing, and how and why they are doing it.

85   There is also a checklist in Appendix 1 that you can use to help you spot workplace transport hazards.

86   A plan of the site can help you see where vehicles are operating, and where any dangers might be.

87   Table 1 lists common types of vehicle and pedestrian movements based on research conducted in the EU. You can use it as the basis for what you look at when you are carrying out this stage of the risk assessment; just add, remove, or change anything that is particular to your work.

Large goods vehicles (including articulated and draw-bar combination vehicles):
❑   transporting raw materials; ❑   transporting other manufacturing materials; ❑   transporting machined or finished products; ❑   deliveries of business supplies (such as stationery, couriers, canteen supplies); ❑   moving products or stock between buildings; ❑   waste removal.
Light goods vehicles:
❑   transporting raw materials; ❑   transporting other manufacturing materials; ❑   transporting machined or finished products; ❑   deliveries of business supplies (such as stationery, couriers, canteen supplies); ❑   cash collection or delivery; ❑   moving products or stock between buildings; ❑   waste removal; ❑   contractors and others (such as maintenance, cleaners, building work, mobile food outlets).
Motorised or other wheeled handling equipment:
❑   movement of raw materials around the site; ❑   movement of components, supplies, stock, etc around the site; ❑   movement of waste material around the site.
Cars:
❑   entering or leaving the premises. Consider staff, clients, other visitors, taxis, couriers and so on; ❑   touring security vehicles.
Vehicles carrying passengers:
❑   consider coaches, minibuses.
Motorcycles and pedal cycles:
❑   entering or leaving the premises; ❑   around storage areas; ❑   couriers.
Other work machinery and plant, including contractors' vehicles:
❑   tractors; ❑   all-terrain vehicles; ❑   backhoes and other earth-moving machinery; ❑   dumpers; ❑   mobile cranes in transit (although lifting operations themselves should not be thought of as workplace transport).
Pedestrians:
❑   entering or leaving the premises; ❑   moving from building to building, or from one work area within a building to another; ❑   moving within storage areas; ❑   moving across vehicle traffic routes; ❑   moving through vehicle manoeuvring areas; ❑   moving from vehicles to buildings, or back (for example, drivers reporting to the site office).

Table 1   Vehicle and pedestrian traffic movements

88   In particular, look for areas where people work around moving vehicles, and where people work on vehicles themselves. You should remember to include every task you can think of, including things:

- that happen at quiet times;
- that don't happen very often (like collecting waste); or
- that take place in a different workplace (such as an employee delivering to a customer's site).

89   Asking any security or other gate staff who enters a site, and when and why, or asking a stores department for a list of which firms deliver when, can help you build up a complete picture of transport activity in your workplace.

90   List all the vehicles that visit your site, and make a note of what they do. Think about when and where these things happen, and what else is happening in that area at the same time. This will make it easier to recognise who might be harmed, in stage 2 of the risk assessment.

91   To identify the hazards, look at each of the work activities associated with transport and ask: 'What are the possible dangers, and what is causing them?'

92   There are four main kinds of accidents that involve workplace transport:

- people being struck by or run over by a vehicle;
- people being struck by something falling from a vehicle;
- people falling from vehicles;
- vehicles overturning.

93   The questions you ask yourself should concentrate on these dangers, and should cover all the aspects of vehicle use in your workplace. Concentrate on things that are likely to cause serious damage, or hurt several people, because these are the more significant hazards. There is a checklist in Appendix 1 to give you an idea of the sort of questions you should be asking. It is based on tasks that often happen around vehicles, and measures to control risks you should be thinking about.

94   When you are looking for transport hazards, you should look at:

- features of your workplace (such as how routes are laid out and whether they are in good condition);
- the vehicles themselves; and
- the actions of the drivers and others who are near to vehicles.

95   Think 'site, vehicle, driver'. You should read whichever parts of this guide are relevant to work that is carried out in your workplace, and use this to help you recognise transport hazards.

96   You should also think carefully about how things could change (for example, at different times of the year or in bad weather). Examples could include:

- drivers being dazzled by strong sunlight at times of the year when the sun is low in the sky;

- bad visibility in a loading area when deliveries are made at night; or
- the effects of strong gusts of wind on people working high up on the outside of vehicles.

97   When you are looking for hazards, you should include any that already have precautions in place to prevent the hazard from harming anyone. For example, if an open-top vehicle is fitted with a system to prevent it from rolling over (or to protect the driver if it does roll over), you should still look to see if there is a possibility that the vehicle will overbalance, and should make a note of any safety measures. Later, you will consider whether any existing precautions are good enough.

98   Employers should ask their drivers, supervisors and any other employees at the site (including contractors and, possibly, visiting drivers) for their views on any problems and what could be done to make the work safer.

99   You may find it helpful to take photographs. You can keep these as part of a recorded risk assessment and to show what hazards and preventive measures have been identified.

Deciding who might be harmed and how

100 For each hazard you identify, you need to decide who might be harmed and how.

101 For hazards involving workplace transport, this is likely to include drivers in particular – both those employed at one site and drivers visiting sites owned by other companies. Also think about all other employees, contractors, subcontractors, customers, part-time employees, cleaners, maintenance staff, visitors and members of the public.

102 Which of these types of people are likely to be near to vehicles, and why?

Evaluating the risks

103 This step is where you decide how serious the risks are, and what you need to do to control them.

104 The risk posed by each hazard is the chance that somebody will be harmed (high or low), and how seriously they might be harmed (seriously or not). High risks are ones where someone is very likely to be harmed or where the harm is likely to be serious (or both).

105 Once you have identified the hazards and who is in danger, you should think about how likely it is that an accident will happen and, if it does, how severe the injury is likely to be. If the hazard is unlikely to harm anyone, the risk will probably be low.

106 Risks are higher for accidents that are very likely to happen, even if the consequences probably wouldn't be too bad. There are not many examples of hazards involving workplace transport that are low risk because transport accidents are usually quite serious, or at least have the potential to be serious.

107 However unlikely it is, if a hazard could cause serious harm, the risk is higher. For example, although it may be unlikely that a person will be struck by a load falling from a vehicle, if it did happen someone could be hurt quite badly, so the risk is high.

108 So risks are higher where accidents are likely, where the consequences are likely to be serious, or both.

109 Once you have decided how much risk a hazard is causing, you can think about controlling the risks. You should ask: 'Has anything been done to reduce this risk, and are the measures enough?'

110 In the first place, if you have not met any general legal duties, or specific legal requirements relating to the hazard, more precautions are needed.

111 If you have already taken measures to reduce particular risks, you will still need to ask whether the other risks are acceptably low. For example, you might decide that as well as setting speed limits on vehicle routes, road humps or other measures are needed to make sure that vehicles do not drive too fast.

112 If you decide that something more needs to be done, you should first try to remove the problem altogether (for example, by restricting vehicle movements to certain parts of the workplace).

113 If you cannot remove the problem, try to reduce the risks.

114 You should always instruct and train employees to take care, to use work equipment safely, and to use personal protective equipment. However, you should not rely on this to keep them safe if there is more you can do.

115 Where possible, change the layout of the workplace or use vehicles with appropriate safety features (for example, have separate pathways for pedestrians, use road humps, or use vehicles with speed limiters). You should also set up safe systems of working (for example, enforce speed limits).

116 It is useful to prioritise the improvement measures you have identified based on the level of risk you have decided each hazard poses, and set a realistic date by which action should be taken.

Record your findings

117 If your organisation employs five or more people (including managers), by law you must record the significant findings of your assessment.

118 This means recording the more significant hazards (usually in writing) and your most important conclusions (for example, 'Risk of dislodged load as a result of low branches – cut back regularly and put up a warning sign').

119 You will find this a very useful part of your risk assessment (no matter how big your organisation is) because it helps you remember what you have found and what you have decided to do.

120 The suggested form in Appendix 2 is a clear way of recording your findings, and it reflects the five-step approach we recommend. There is also an example of how a risk assessment could look, to help you when you do your own.

121 You must also tell your employees, including any safety representatives, about your findings. You can do this more easily with a written record.

Review the risk assessment

122 You should review the risk assessment from time to time, to check that it is still relevant. Each risk assessment should include a date for when a review is due, which should take account of the type of work and the speed of changes, which are likely to be different for every workplace.

123 Sooner or later you are likely to introduce new vehicles or change the traffic routes, or the nature of the work activities relating to vehicles may change, which can lead to new hazards.

124 You should assess risks before you make any significant changes. This will help keep risks as low as possible from the moment the changes are introduced. You must consult employees either directly or through elected safety representatives if the changes could substantially affect their health and safety. See *Control, co-operation and consultation* (paragraphs 126-153) for more information about consulting employees.

125 You should always keep the risk assessment up to date with working practices and equipment, no matter what reviews may be due 'soon'.

Organising for safety

126 Establishing responsibilities and relationships is a very important part of securing safe working practices and promoting a culture of safety.

127 To secure and maintain a safe workplace, everyone from senior managers to individual employees needs to be aware of their individual responsibilities for safety, and act accordingly.

Control, co-operation and consultation

128 The main aspects to controlling safety in the workplace are as follows:

Take overall responsibility
129 Employers need to take responsibility for safety and show their commitment by example and in everyday decisions. For example:

- by holding regular (weekly or monthly) meetings with employees and safety representatives (if you have these), to discuss current work activities and associated safety issues. Meetings are usually more effective if they have a chairperson, a clear agenda, and when actions and deadlines are recorded in minutes;
- by making regular and noticeable tours of the workplace, including inspections of vehicles, roadways and behaviour, to check that there are no obvious hazards in the workplace and that safe working practices are being followed. You should report on both good and bad features of managing risks in the workplace; and
- by making sure that formal or informal work-related discussions with employees always include safety issues.

130 A clear and simple procedure for reporting faults, hazards and incidents (often known as a 'near-miss reporting scheme') can help prevent serious accidents.

131 An accident reporting system is essential for you to meet your legal duties to report some accidents. It is also valuable for monitoring how effective measures to prevent accidents are, and making sure that all accidents are reported to managers. However, it is important that managers do not use the accident reporting system to blame people as this may discourage employees from using it.

Allocate specific responsibilities
132 Responsibilities for health and safety management need to be clearly allocated. It is vital that all employees, contractors, subcontractors, visiting drivers, maintenance staff and other workers clearly understand their

responsibilities for maintaining a safe workplace and safe working practices.

133 There are various ways of achieving this, for example by:

- including safety responsibilities in employees' job descriptions, and in contracts with contractors and companies whose employees drive on site;
- including safety issues and responsibilities in the information, instruction and training given to people who are new to the workplace;
- raising safety issues and responsibilities while supervising employees and being in daily contact with them; and
- displaying safety notices or bulletins, risk assessment findings and the results of safety inspections, where people can clearly see them.

134 Consider dividing up the workplace (including car parks, access roads, weighbridges, lay-bys and other areas) into areas where managers are responsible for carrying out risk assessments, taking action, and maintaining and repairing features. These areas should then be shown on a drawing that everyone has easy access to, and should cover the whole area of the workplace.

Enforcement
135 However responsibility for transport safety is arranged, it is important that people are accountable. Employers and managers need to make sure that everyone is held responsible for their duties, mainly through supervision. Performance agreements, appraisals and so on should include safety-related responsibilities, for managers and supervisors as well as other workers. It is important that there are clear penalties for poor performance, and also rewards for good performance.

136 Supervision is an essential part of monitoring safe working. The level of supervision should reflect how serious the risks involved are and the ability of employees to avoid them. Even where risks are low, some supervision will always be needed to make sure that standards are being maintained.

137 There are also other ways of making sure people meet their duties. Security systems (such as patrols, gate staff and camera systems) can be a very effective way of checking that workplace rules are being followed.

138 Gate staff in particular can be a very effective way of making sure visitors receive safety information before they enter the site.

139 There will usually need to be a clear system of penalties if anyone fails to maintain standards or follow safe working practices. For employees, there are usually disciplinary procedures, with the possibility of dismissal. For contractors, there may be financial penalties or termination of their contract (or both).

140 Authorising specific people to operate certain vehicles, or to carry out vehicle-related activities (such as maintenance) can help employers or managers control risks.

141 Employers need to make sure that all managers, employees, contractors and visiting drivers are able to do their work in a proper way (one which protects their own safety and that of other people).

142 In a large organisation, senior managers need to be satisfied that managers and supervisors involved in day-to-day work activities are able to secure safe working practices and a safe workplace. They need to be able to:

■ control risks;
■ communicate effectively to maintain a flow of information on safety, in both directions;
■ encourage the people they are responsible for to co-operate; and
■ organise activity in a way that secures and maintains a safe working environment.

143 In all organisations, those in charge need to make sure wherever possible that employees, contractors and visitors are carrying out their work activities in a safe and responsible way. For workplace transport, this is likely to include checking training and previous experience, knowledge, abilities and general fitness for tasks they need to do (for example, are they completely sober and in control?).

144 Those in charge will need to be able and willing to provide information, instruction, supervision and constructive feedback to employees on their safety performance.

145 There are two main ways of making sure people are competent for a job, which should be used together:

■ **make sure new recruits are competent.** Have effective recruitment and placement procedures to make sure that all those employed at the workplace (including managers) have the relevant knowledge and experience to be able to do their jobs safely, or can gain these on the job or through training. See *Choosing drivers* (paragraphs 631-641) for more information about choosing competent operators;
■ **make sure existing employees are competent.** Provide information, instruction and training to maintain or improve employees' competence, particularly where changes in staff, equipment or procedures are planned. This should take account of employees' abilities and experience.

146 By law, employees must take reasonable care of their own health and safety and that of others who may be affected by what they do at work.

147 By law, employees must co-operate with their employers, so they can meet with their health and safety responsibilities.

148 Good communication within an organisation helps secure and maintain a safe workplace.

149 It is important that there are strong lines of communication, so that everyone is clear about their health and safety responsibilities and any changes are quickly put into practice across the whole organisation.

150 Information that needs to be communicated includes:

■ the organisation's safety policy, and what it means in practice;
■ who has which safety responsibilities;
■ details of safe working practices that should be followed;
■ details of where employees and other workers can get more information, instruction or training on particular areas of their work activities (this should be easily available – for example, in an area where drivers or other workers take regular breaks);
■ feedback to employees on how well they have followed safe working practices; and
■ communicating with other employers – for example, agreeing safety precautions and responsibilities for visiting vehicles delivering or collecting goods.

151 You should encourage everyone in the workplace (including contractors) to take an active interest in safety issues. Everyone should have the chance to express their views or concerns to those in charge of the workplace and the people they work with.

152 As well as making good sense, consulting employees on health and safety matters is a legal requirement. If your organisation has safety representatives who have been appointed by a trade union that your organisation recognises, by law you must consult them. If there are no safety representatives, you should consult the employees themselves or any health and safety representative they have elected.

153 Employers have a legal duty to set up a health and safety committee when two or more safety representatives from recognised trade unions ask them to do so. A health and safety committee can be an effective way of encouraging everyone in the workplace (including visitors delivering or collecting goods) to formally co-operate in carrying out their health and safety responsibilities.

Contractors

154 Where contractors or subcontractors are employed, the site operator or principal employer should make sure that they fit in with the overall work scheme, without increasing risks unnecessarily.

155 The site operator or principal employer will need to give the contractor appropriate health and safety information on

the work to be carried out, so that the work can be done safely. For example, the information should be about:

- the workplace;
- the routes to be used;
- the vehicles and equipment on site;
- specific hazards; and
- other people on site, including other contractors, visiting drivers and so on.

156 The site controller and any contractors due to work on the site should agree what needs to be done to ensure vehicle safety before the contractor starts work on site.

157 If anyone has doubts about the proposed safety arrangements, they should take all reasonable steps to improve the arrangements before the work starts. The precautions and level of co-operation needed will depend on the particular risks involved.

158 The site operator or principal employer should check that the contractor and (through the contractor) any subcontractor is suitable, in terms of health and safety standards. Check, for example:

- that the contractor chooses and trains employees to the necessary standards and that they are suitably competent;
- that, on previous contracts, the contractor has followed safe working practices (where possible, check the contractor's accident and ill-health record); and
- that any vehicles the contractor uses in the workplace are suitable for their intended purpose and are, and will continue to be, properly maintained.

159 You will also need to make the contractor fully aware of the penalties they will face if they don't maintain standards or if they fail to follow safe working practices.

160 You may need to make sure that following good health and safety practice and any specific site regulations are set out in the contract. This could explain the penalties for breaking safe working practices (unsafe working means breaching the terms of a contract) and should benefit the contractor – providing them with protection if they need to refuse to work for health and safety reasons.

161 It is important to maintain a system to adequately supervise the contractor's work.

162 Licensing systems can be a useful way of controlling the work activities of contractors and subcontractors. Licences to operate on site are issued for certain periods, and are only renewed if contractors have behaved satisfactorily.

163 When a contractor employs subcontractors, the contractor can clearly use similar checks and supervision to control the subcontractors' work. The site operator will usually need evidence from the contractor that adequate controls over subcontractors are in place.

164 Despite these precautions, contractors should be in no doubt that they are responsible for their own employees and their activities.

Visiting drivers

165 Some of the checks and procedures we explain above for contractors will also apply to visiting drivers.

166 It is important to make sure that visiting drivers are aware of the workplace layout, the route they need to take, and relevant safe working practices (for example, for parking and unloading).

167 You should take account of the fact that delivery drivers may never have visited the site before, and may only be on site for a short time.

168 They should not have to enter potentially dangerous areas to move to or from their vehicles or places they need to go, such as the site office, or toilet or washroom facilities.

169 The employer at a workplace should work and co-operate as fully as possible with the employers of visiting drivers, to co-ordinate the measures that need to be taken for both employers and their employees to meet their health and safety responsibilities. For example, employers should communicate to:

- provide safe access to a vehicle for loading or unloading;
- provide suitable equipment (for example, for drivers delivering at retail outlets) to unload safely; and
- make sure that vehicles and the type of ground they have to use are suitable for safe working.

170 You should consider printing site rules, directions, maps and approach information (for example, narrow routes, weak bridges and so on) on the back of order forms and invoices, allowing visiting drivers to know what to expect before arriving on site.

171 See *Deliveries – communication* (paragraphs 203-227) for more information about communicating about workplace transport activities in shared premises.

Shared workplaces

172 The law places some very specific duties on employers who share workplaces. Wherever two or more employers share a workplace (whether temporarily or permanently), each employer must:

- co-operate with the other employers so that they can meet their health and safety duties;
- take all reasonable steps to co-ordinate the measures they take to meet their legal duties with those taken by other employers; and
- take all reasonable steps to tell the other employers about risks to their employees' health and safety as a result of their work activities.

173 This legal obligation also applies to self-employed people working at a shared workplace.

174 The type of co-ordination needed will depend on the circumstances, but all employers and self-employed people involved will need to satisfy themselves that they are meeting their legal duties.

175 Normally, the site operator or a main employer controls the worksite. In these cases, they will need to take responsibility for co-ordinating health and safety measures:

■ mainly through discussion and by getting information from the smaller employers;
■ by asking for their agreement to site-wide arrangements, whether new or established;
■ by all other employers taking responsibility to co-operate.

176 Where employees enter a different workplace (for example, to make a delivery or collect goods), you might find it helpful to think of that workplace as being shared.

177 Vehicles on which employees of more than one company are working are also considered shared workplaces, even if it is only for a brief period (for example, during loading, unloading or sheeting). Both employers are responsible for the safety of their own employees and those of other companies involved.

178 Anyone involved in working together like this should agree at the start who will be responsible for what, including safety. Sharing a vehicle could mean risks are different and the law may mean that they have to be assessed again.

179 If there is no employer in overall control, individual employers and self-employed people will need to find a way of agreeing joint arrangements (for example, by appointing a health and safety supervisor or co-ordinator, or setting up a health and safety committee).

180 Appointing a health and safety supervisor or co-ordinator is likely to be the most effective way of:

■ making sure there is co-operation and co-ordination; and
■ exchanging information efficiently, so that all employers can meet their health and safety duties.

181 However joint arrangements are made, everyone on the site should support and follow any resulting procedures or regulations. Clear penalties for failing to do so should be established as soon as possible.

Deliveries – general safety

182 Deliveries and collections are essential to business, but can be some of the most dangerous transport activities that take place. A significant number of transport accidents in the workplace take place during deliveries.

183 Hazards can include:

■ being struck by a vehicle;
■ injuries when loads are moved by hand;
■ falls from vehicles; and

■ risks from using cranes or other lifting equipment such as lorry loaders.

184 The specific risks relating to hazardous chemicals or other dangerous loads are not covered by this guidance.

185 Generally, parking and loading or unloading should be off the road and pavement, well away from members of the public. Loading or unloading over the pavement should be avoided, but where this is not possible a specific risk assessment should be carried out for the task.

186 If a delivery vehicle parks up on a public road outside a supplier's or recipient's premises, any loading or unloading is still covered by health and safety law, and all of the normal duties of employers and employees apply. In particular, there can be risks to the safety of members of the public who drive or walk near the loading or unloading.

187 Delivery drivers should try to park their vehicle so that the side of the delivery vehicle with the easiest access to the load is towards the workplace, instead of towards the road. This is to reduce the amount of work that takes place in the flow of traffic, and near members of the public.

188 If other ways of making reversing safe are not effective enough, the employer whose premises are being used may need to consider providing a competent and authorised signaller (banksman), with appropriate high-visibility equipment and using agreed hand signals. See chapter *Reversing* for more information about using banksmen.

189 A signaller working in these conditions will need to give priority to public traffic (both pedestrian and vehicles) because the signaller will have no authority to stop traffic on the road. If cones or barriers are to be used, employers should discuss this with the local police and the highway authority. Pedestrians should not be directed onto the road.

190 If lift trucks are being used, it is important that drivers and their employers are aware of any increased risk of overturn that would result from driving them over kerbs or on a road camber that might make them unstable.

191 If articulated vehicles are being coupled or uncoupled, drivers should have been instructed on how to park each type of vehicle they use, as there can be significant differences and misunderstandings. Semi-trailer parking brakes and cab handbrakes should always be used, and the emergency brakes should never be relied on. See chapter *Coupling and uncoupling* for more information.

192 The delivery driver plays an important part in delivery safety, and is often the person injured in delivery or collection accidents. The driver should receive adequate safety information for each delivery or collection beforehand.

193 Everyone involved should set up simple, well-understood systems for reporting any vehicle accidents, incidents, near misses and other safety concerns during deliveries and collections, and exchanging information with everyone else.

194 Everyone should be encouraged to report incidents and concerns and appropriate action should be taken where reports are made.

195 Drivers may be faced with unexpected situations. Employers should train drivers in general safety precautions to take when visiting sites, in particular concerning the risks involved in loading and unloading.

196 As well as training, providing drivers with simple delivery safety checklists may help them check that reasonable precautions have been taken, and help them decide if it is reasonable for them to refuse to continue with a particular delivery or collection.

197 Hauliers (or other load transport companies) should make sure that any agency drivers they use are familiar with their arrangements for delivery safety.

198 Although responsibility for safety will remain with the employer, suppliers and recipients should consider authorising an employee who will be present to permit and manage loading or unloading. That employee should be allowed to refuse or stop the work if safe working practices are not available or being followed, including dealing with unsafe loads or loads that have shifted in transit. The person responsible should be confident that a decision to refuse delivery would be supported by their employer. See chapter *Loading and unloading, and load safety* for more advice about dealing with loads that have shifted in transit.

199 Similarly, if you employ delivery drivers, they should be given clear instructions about what to do if they are not satisfied with the arrangements for safety at a particular site. You should let your employees know that they are authorised to refuse or stop loading or unloading for safety reasons, and when you arrange the delivery you should tell the recipient about this authority. Everyone should be aware of what to do if they are not happy with safety arrangements (including who to report concerns to). The delivery staff should be confident that a decision to refuse delivery would be supported by their employer.

200 A safe system of work should be followed during deliveries. Where both delivery drivers and site workers are involved, it should be clear to everyone who has priority for controlling the operation at any one time:

■ when the driver is manoeuvring the delivery vehicle, it should be clear that they have priority;
■ where site workers then need to access the vehicle, there should be a clear moment for handing priority over. Only the delivery driver can decide when they are satisfied that the vehicle will not need to move again until it has been loaded, and when priority can safely pass to the site workers;
■ site workers should then be able to tell when it is safe for priority to be handed back to the delivery driver for departure. The driver should not be allowed to leave until they have been told it is safe to do so.

201 Where visiting vehicles have had problems before, or where deliveries or collections will take place regularly and special risks are likely, it may be necessary for a manager to visit and assess the risks involved and agree precautions.

202 There is more information about safety during unloading in chapter *Loading and unloading, and load safety.*

Deliveries – communication

203 Several companies are likely to be involved in a delivery, typically:

■ a supplier sending the goods;
■ a carrier – the company carrying the goods (often a haulier); and
■ a recipient – the company receiving the goods.

204 As with other areas of workplace transport, employers have a legal duty to take all 'reasonably practicable' steps to ensure the safety of everyone affected by their work activities and on their premises, and to co-operate with other employers to ensure health and safety.

205 Many delivery and collection accidents could be prevented if there was better co-operation between the people involved. A lack of any agreement about 'who is responsible for what' in terms of safety is a common factor in delivery accidents.

Case study 1

A site employee suffered severe injuries when he was trapped against a doorframe by a lift truck, driven by an untrained operator.

When a delivery arrived earlier than expected, there wasn't a trained lift truck operator available on site. The delivery driver decided to operate the site lift truck himself to unload. He reversed into pallets, over-corrected and reversed into the site employee.

The site operator should have made sure that only authorised people could use the lift truck. The site operator and the driver's employer should have liaised and agreed procedures for unloading deliveries. These procedures should have included fixing a time for vehicles to arrive with deliveries. The driver should not have tried to operate a site vehicle without authorisation.

206 In most work situations, the safety of an employee is mainly the responsibility of their employer. However, to deliver or collect goods, employees have to visit premises controlled by others. The safety of everyone at these premises, including visitors, is in the hands of the person in charge of the site – the supplier for collections or the recipient for deliveries.

207 This overlap can cause dangerous misunderstandings. Everyone involved needs to exchange information about the main risks involved, and agree who will do what to control risks.

208 By law, if two or more employers share a workplace, even temporarily, they must co-operate to make sure they all meet their legal duties.

209 The number of people involved and how often deliveries take place will affect the extent of arrangements between companies involved in a delivery.

210 All parties involved in deliveries should exchange and agree information to make sure goods can be delivered and collected safely. Even for a 'one-off' delivery, everyone involved should communicate to make sure safety responsibilities have been met.

211 The main purposes of good communication about deliveries and collections are:

■ to make expectations clear;
■ to ask others involved whether they can meet these expectations; and
■ if expectations cannot be met, to agree what to do. If an agreement cannot be reached on how significant safety issues will be dealt with, the delivery or collection should not take place.

212 Everyone involved in a collection or a delivery should achieve the following three aims:

■ to send out safety information on deliveries and collections to other parties involved in the supply chain;
■ to receive safety information on deliveries and collections from other parties involved in the supply chain;
■ to agree a safe delivery plan between everyone involved.

213 It is useful to share the following information:

■ restrictions on the type or size of vehicle the site can safely handle;
■ restrictions on when goods should be delivered or collected;
■ safe approach routes to the site, especially if nearby one-way systems, low or weak bridges, narrow roads, awkward access and other features could cause problems for visiting vehicles;
■ a site plan or sketch showing parking, where the reception is, the route to take through the site, and where loading or unloading areas are;
■ where visiting vehicles should park when arriving, where drivers should report to and any other instructions for the driver;
■ procedures that visiting drivers need to follow – for example, wearing high-visibility vests, limits on using mobile phones, restrictions on reversing or conditions for reversing such as using a banksman;
■ what to do if a load appears to have shifted dangerously in transit;
■ the point at which the visiting driver will give permission for their vehicle to be unloaded, and how everyone will clearly understand this handover (before this time, site staff should keep clear of the vehicle, and during unloading the driver should keep clear of the vehicle);

■ information about general loading and unloading procedures, including who will have overall responsibility, the types of vehicle and machinery available, the weights or volumes equipment can lift and storage areas;
■ loading and unloading safety procedures, such as where drivers should wait during delivery, times or places at which deliveries have been banned, safety and personal protective equipment that must be used;
■ what visiting drivers or site staff should do if they are not satisfied with safety arrangements for the delivery or collection (for example, who to report concerns to); and
■ contact details for the other people involved in case there are problems.

214 You should consider (and, if possible, agree) delivery safety arrangements before you take or place orders. This will reduce the risk of accidents and the risk of wasting time and money when a delivery is delayed or has to be sent back because a site can't handle the load or the vehicle carrying it.

215 An agreement about delivery or collection safety arrangements can take different forms.

216 It will often be possible to include safety arrangements in ordering procedures, to make sure you take them into account and keep paperwork down as much as possible.

217 A very effective way to reduce the amount of time taken making safety arrangements with different suppliers, hauliers and recipients is to develop a general safety information sheet or pack which you can send to anyone in the supply chain, along with any specific safety arrangements for individual deliveries. This should include the sort of information set out in paragraph 213.

218 Trade associations can consider developing model delivery plans on behalf of their industries.

219 If a site will regularly receive deliveries, it may be reasonable for suppliers or carriers to send an appropriately trained member of staff to sites beforehand, to assess the delivery risks involved and to agree procedures, equipment and other safety measures.

220 If a recipient regularly receives similar deliveries from a particular supplier or carrier, everyone should agree a written delivery plan. If something about a particular delivery may make it unsafe to rely on the usual plan, the delivery should not start until different arrangements have been agreed.

221 When recipients, suppliers and carriers deal with each other on a 'last-minute, one-off' basis, it would usually be considered 'reasonably practicable' to exchange basic delivery safety information, and agree on the main precautions, at the time an order is placed.

222 In some situations other parties may be involved. For example, a customer (the recipient) may place an order with a supplier, the supplier might arrange for a third company (another supplier) to provide the goods, and the third company might arrange for a fourth company (the carrier) to

make the delivery. Complicated arrangements like this can easily go wrong because of communication problems.

223 You should consider the dangers of this before entering into these arrangements. If a delivery accident happens, everyone in the relevant part of the supply chain might be asked to show that they took all reasonable steps to co-operate to achieve safety.

224 Visiting drivers have been known to travel with children or pets, which might pose risks to health and safety in work environments. You should discourage this, and any non-essential people or animals should be kept in a clear and safe place at all times (for example, pets should not be allowed to leave the cab).

225 If drivers are likely to have difficulty understanding English, plans and information may need to be available in languages the drivers use. Pictures can also be useful in helping to communicate across language barriers.

226 Sites that are often visited by foreign drivers may have other considerations. Foreign drivers may have been exposed to different sign standards, and are likely to be more familiar with 'kilometres per hour' speed limits than signs in miles per hour.

227 Foreign drivers are also likely to have different visibility from their cabs (if their vehicles are left-hand drive) and are also less likely to be familiar with the controls for workplace equipment such as lift trucks.

Members of the public

228 If the public have access to the premises, routes for public use should:

- where possible, be separate from work activities ('segregation'); and
- be as close as possible to the place they want to go (for example, to visit a farm or factory shop, toilets, refreshment areas or ticket offices).

229 Clear signs at the entrance should direct visitors to a car park with safe access to the area they are visiting, and should show which traffic routes they can use. See chapter *A safe site* for more information about the principles you should consider to keep members of the public and others safe from the risks of workplace transport.

230 You should take account of elderly or disabled people, the distractions of dealing with families, and lack of familiarity by customers with the hazards and risks of the workplace.

Case study 2

An elderly shopper was crushed to death by a lift truck at a DIY store.

During prosecution, the firm claimed that the day of the accident was an isolated incident and control of lift truck movements at the store did not comply with the company's own guidelines. However, CCTV tapes seized during the investigation showed that lift trucks were used in public areas of the store on a number of occasions during the six months prior to the accident, and in a manner unsuitable for public areas.

The prosecution was successful, and the firm was fined £550 000 with £250 000 costs.

---

231 Retail and wholesale premises are obviously used by members of the public. If you are in control of this sort of site, you should make every effort to provide separate delivery areas, although this is not always possible at existing sites. If vehicles have to move through areas used by the public, it may be possible to time deliveries outside opening hours. You should use banksmen as a last resort to make sure members of the public are kept clear.

232 Members of the public should not be allowed into areas where lift trucks are operating. If a lift truck needs access to a shop floor (or an outside yard) during opening hours, there should be a written procedure setting out precautions to be taken. These should include fencing off areas used by the truck and announcements to tell shoppers to keep out of the barricaded area.

233 In ports and docks, you should take account of language difficulties when you tell members of the public about safe behaviour or transport issues.

Public roads as workplaces

234 Although driving on public roads is not normally considered 'workplace transport', you should make sure that your risk assessment includes other work that takes place on or near public roads.

235 Both workers and members of the public need to be protected from risks caused both by the work and by traffic nearby. In particular, the risk assessment should identify any protective equipment that is necessary, such as clothing that is suitable for the conditions workers will be exposed to (for example, weatherproof), footwear, gloves, and head, eye and hearing protection.

236 Employers also need to make sure that 'safe systems of work' are available and used for work on public roads, as they would be for other workplaces. See paragraph 68 in *Phrases and meanings* for a description of safe systems of work.

237 See *What is workplace transport?* (paragraphs 18-24) for advice about the difference between 'workplace transport' and 'work-related road safety'.

A safe site

The workplace in general

238 A well-designed and maintained workplace will make transport accidents less likely.

239 This guidance should provide enough information for you to recognise common transport hazards related to the layout and features of the site, and to think about things you can do to reduce risks resulting from these hazards.

240 Every site is different and each site is likely to present hazards and risks we do not mention here. These should be recognised in a thorough risk assessment, and controlled accordingly. Often, small and quite cheap things will make a lot of difference. You should make sure that lights are adequate and working, potholes are filled, markings and signs are clear, spills are cleaned up quickly, and so on.

241 You can get more detailed information on site design from other sources, including the Freight Transport Association guide *Designing for Deliveries*,[8] other industry guidance, British Standards Institute publications, and professional civil engineers and transport planners.

242 If transport is used in a workplace, it is important that vehicles and pedestrians are kept separate wherever possible, and are able to move around each other and do their work safely. This is known as 'segregation'.

243 People do not only need to be segregated from vehicles that are travelling. They also need to be kept separate from the area that a vehicle moves through when it is working – for example, the area that the body of an excavator moves through when it is working.

244 By law, the workplace must be maintained in an efficient state, in efficient working order and in good repair. 'Efficient' here relates to health and safety, not to productivity or economy.

245 To make sure that a workplace is managed efficiently in this sense, it is important that those responsible for it have a good understanding of how work is carried out on site. This will involve understanding how pedestrians and vehicles use the space around them.

246 When you are thinking about features of your site, it is important that you know what sort of vehicles move around your site and where they are going. You can then think about:

- how much room vehicles need to move safely;
- whether pedestrians are kept safely clear of vehicles;
- how much drivers can see when the vehicle is moving; and
- whether drivers can get to and from the driving position safely.

247 As a rule, your site should allow plenty of room for all of the types of vehicle that are used in the normal course of work to move and work safely. Wherever possible, you should also allow for other vehicles that might need to move around the workplace, such as emergency vehicles.

248 You should bear in mind that drivers and vehicles rarely behave perfectly, so you should allow for safety margins wherever possible (for example, allow for oversteering within reason). You can find out more about this under *Traffic routes* in paragraphs 258-318.

249 To allow people and vehicles to move safely, the best approach is to separate vehicles from pedestrians entirely (segregation). You can find out more about segregating vehicles and pedestrians under *Traffic routes* (paragraphs 258-318) and *Pedestrians and cyclists* (paragraphs 371-392).

250 Another important part of site design is to improve visibility for drivers and pedestrians.

251 Because drivers often have trouble seeing behind their vehicle while they are reversing, one of the best ways to improve safety is to make sure vehicles do not have to reverse. This is best achieved by using one-way systems with drive-through loading areas.

252 One-way systems also help pedestrians know which direction vehicles are likely to be coming from, and it is easier to arrange routes so that they allow for good visibility around corners and at crossing points. One-way systems should normally work clockwise around a site, as this is the direction most drivers will expect.

Case study 3

An employee was injured by a 360° excavator, which was operating in a poorly organised scrapyard.

The employee was removing a part from a vehicle when the reversing excavator, which had been converted for use as a vehicle grab, hit him and the track went over his right leg. The excavator was not fitted with devices to improve visibility from the cab, such as rear-mounted convex mirrors or CCTV, and the driver had not received formal excavator training. The excavator was working within 3 or 4 m of the injured worker on a daily basis, had knocked him once before and would often lift scrap cars over his head.

After the accident, the firm reorganised the yard and fenced off the area where employees were manually dismantling vehicles. The excavator is now used in a pedestrian-free area.

253 You should also try to make sure that any fittings in your workplace can be operated from a safe place. In the case of drivers, this is best achieved by allowing them to stay in their vehicle cab (where it is safe for them to do so), or to stay well clear of operations. Examples would include:

- gate or barrier buttons, intercom systems and security points that can be reached from the driving position of vehicles using the site;
- fill gauges or similar indicators that can be read without workers needing to climb structures or vehicles; and
- controls for dock levellers that can be used from several feet clear of the moving parts.

Figure 2 Key pad accessible from driving position

254 Landlords can play a very important role in how tenants are able to arrange their site.

255 You may need to work with your landlord to provide safety features on site, and to make sure you have the right to do this when you negotiate your lease.

256 Just as professional advice is often needed in legal or financial matters, you may also need professional advice to properly plan vehicle movements, site layout, traffic control features and other civil engineering. The information here should help you recognise common hazards and plan what you can do to control them, but you should ask for professional help when you need it.

257 There are laws that govern some aspects of the way a workplace is managed, and some deal particularly with traffic movements ('traffic' here means the movement of both people and vehicles). This guidance sets out whether something included is necessary by law.

Traffic routes

258 By law, every workplace must be organised so that pedestrians and vehicles can circulate safely.

259 The law also requires that workplace traffic routes must be suitable for the people and vehicles using them and, where vehicles and pedestrians share a traffic route, there must be enough separation between them (segregation).

260 These are the general principles you should follow when you are deciding on the layout of your traffic routes, or when asking yourself whether they are suitable:

- routes should be wide enough for the safe movement of the largest vehicle allowed to use them, including visiting vehicles;
- they should be made of a suitable material, and should be constructed soundly enough to safely bear the loads that will pass over them;
- there should be enough routes to prevent overcrowding;
- plan traffic routes to give the safest route between places where vehicles have to call. Avoid vehicle routes passing close to:
  - dangerous items unless they are well protected (for example, fuel or chemical tanks or pipes); and
  - any unprotected edge from which vehicles could fall, or where they could become unstable, such as unfenced edges of elevated weighbridges, loading bays or excavations; and
  - any unprotected and vulnerable features (for example, anything that is likely to collapse or be left in a dangerous condition if hit by a vehicle, such as cast iron columns).

261 Routes will need to be wide enough to allow for developments that have taken place over the last few decades in how materials are handled, such as pedestrian-operated pallet handlers.

262 People count as 'traffic', so you should consider people on foot and the types of work equipment they might use.

263 You need to consider pallet handlers, stackers and other handling equipment that pedestrians use. You might have to decide on traffic routes around the workplace before this equipment is used regularly.

264 Make entrances and gateways wide enough. Where possible, there should be enough space to allow two vehicles to pass each other without causing a blockage. If gates or barriers are to be left open, they should be secured in position.

265 Routes should also be wide enough to allow vehicles to pass oncoming or parked vehicles safely without leaving the route.

266 The law that requires traffic routes to be wide enough for traffic to circulate freely came into effect on 1 January 1993, so it only applies to routes laid out on or after that date. On traffic routes that existed before 1 January 1993, where it is not practical to widen the road you should introduce one-way systems, passing places, traffic management systems or restrictions on parking where necessary.

267 It is important that the people responsible for the site understand the size and turning abilities of the vehicles that use the site, as well as the standard of visibility from the cab and in what ways this might be poor. We explain a way to identify what types of vehicle are used in your workplace in the chapter *Managing the risks*.

268 Vehicles that use public roads in the UK cannot be larger than a certain size, and have to be able to turn in a certain amount of space.

269 Straight routes used by road-going vehicles should usually be at least 3.5 m wide in each direction, although where speeds are slow, traffic is light, and very wide vehicles or overhanging loads are unlikely, this may be reduced to 3 m.

270 Large vehicles, and especially articulated and drawbar combinations, often need to perform complicated manoeuvres to turn safely, because the trailers swing out behind the tractive unit. This often involves taking the tractive unit in a larger circle than a car would follow.

271 Most vehicles using European roads have to be able to turn within a certain amount of space. This is the space between an inner circle of 5.3 m radius and an outer circle of 12.5 m radius. Figure 3 shows how this works.

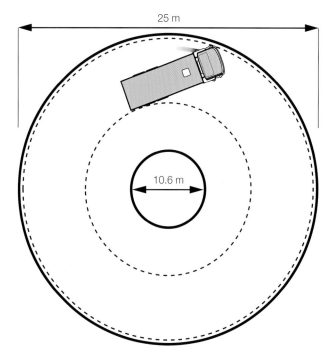

Note: *Vehicle shown for illustration purposes only*

Figure 3 A vehicle needs to be able to turn in a full circle within the solid lines, which represent the turning corridor required by European law

272 If large goods vehicles are using your site, you need to make routes wide enough for them to manoeuvre safely and to pass each other with room to spare wherever possible. For more information about how large vehicles move, you should read the Freight Transport Association publication *Designing for Deliveries*.[8]

273 You should also remember that working on a slope will change how well a vehicle is able to manoeuvre, usually meaning more space is needed.

274 You should consider the height of vehicles (and their loads) that are operating on your site. You should then use this information to make decisions about how much overhead space they need to move around and work safely.

275 There is no maximum height for road vehicles in the UK, but they tend to be less than 4.5 m tall. One exception to this is tipper vehicles, which can be much taller than this when they are raised and need a lot of clearance overhead to do this. There is more information about tipping safely in the chapter *Tipping*. When they are driving normally, tipper vehicles are usually shorter than 4.5 m.

276 You should measure and record the vertical clearance under overhead obstructions on routes. The measurement should take account of any underhanging lighting, ventilation or other service features, which are often added after the initial design.

Figure 4 This overhead structure is signposted with a height restriction

277 If possible, routes used by road vehicles should allow for 5.1 m clearance (which is the normal height of UK motorway bridges). You should remember that if there is a steep ramp running down to an overhead obstruction (for example, when entering a building), the effective height could be reduced for longer vehicles. Figure 5 shows how this happens.

278 Clearance for goods vehicles may change with raising or lowering the mid-lift axle, if this is a vehicle feature.

279 A change to the level of the driving surface could also affect clearance. If a route is resurfaced, you may need to take measurements again.

280 Any potentially dangerous obstructions (such as overhead electric cables or pipes containing flammable or hazardous chemicals) need to be protected using goalposts, height gauge posts or barriers.

281 Routes should also avoid anything that might catch on or dislodge a load.

282 You should give clear warnings of any limited width or headroom, both in advance and at the obstruction itself. See *Signs, signals and markings* in paragraphs 393-402 for more information about hazard signs.

283 Vehicles that are too large or heavy to use a route need to be prevented from trying to do so.

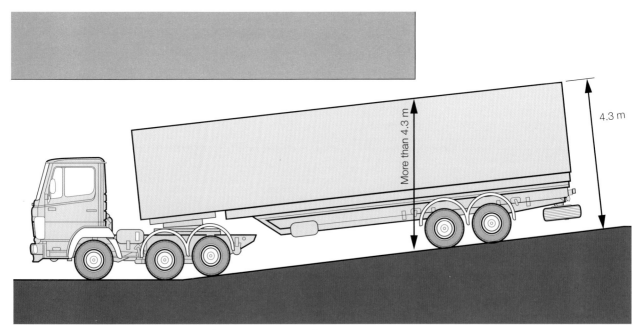

Note: Vehicle and measurements shown for illustration purposes only

Figure 5 Slopes can make a difference to the amount of clearance a vehicle needs

284 It is better to restrict vehicles at a place where they can choose another route, or at least where they will not need to reverse or manoeuvre in a tight space when they find out that they can't go ahead. Width and height restriction posts can be very effective for this.

A sign like this can be used to provide advance warning of a restriction or prohibition ahead

This sign should be used to show that there is no entry for vehicular traffic

This sign should be used to show that there is no left turn for vehicles

This sign should be used to show that there is no right turn for vehicles

Figure 6 Access signs

285 See *Construction of traffic routes* (paragraphs 319-337), for more information about vehicle weights, and *Signs, signals and markings* (paragraphs 393-402) for more information about signs for hazards.

286 You need to understand how much space is needed for the vehicles that move around your particular site, and make decisions about how much space they need.

287 Steep gradients can make handling vehicles difficult, especially if the surface is made slippery (for example by a spill or by poor weather). Slopes also affect how easily spills can be contained, and how easy it is to manage wheeled objects such as waste containers, roll cages or pallet handlers.

288 Some vehicles can become unstable on slopes. Examples include some lift trucks, raised-tipper lorries, raised-body tankers involved in transferring powder or bulk solids, and vehicles with a trailer containing liquids (such as a bowser or a slurry tanker) but without effective baffles to stop the liquid surging around.

289 Steep slopes can also make loads less stable, especially if they are stacked or if they are unstable anyway (for example, wire coils or reels, barrels). You should take care that loads are not able to move dangerously if they are being moved on slopes.

290 Even where vehicles can safely use sloping surfaces, slopes steeper than 1 in 10 should be avoided.

291 There is information about the construction of slopes on traffic routes in *Construction of traffic routes* in paragraphs 319-337.

> ## Case study 4
>
> A company was fined a total of £20 000 after a reversing vehicle at its site killed a delivery driver.
>
> The driver was delivering goods when the accident happened. Standing by the side of his lorry after overseeing the removal of its load, he was struck by a reversing lift truck. He died instantly.
>
> The company had failed to carry out a suitable risk assessment for the movement of loads at the site. This would have shown the need for lift trucks to avoid reversing for long distances, and that drivers should be removed from the danger area. They should have installed suitable barriers to prevent pedestrians gaining access to areas where vehicles were working, and established a formal system for supervising site visitors.
>
> It had also become common practice for heavy goods vehicles to reverse onto the site from the public highway, putting pedestrians at further risk of being struck by vehicles.
>
> Since the death, the company has issued health and safety guidelines to all visitors and has improved the supervision of vehicle and pedestrian movements on site.

292 In workplaces where one-way systems are not practical, it may be appropriate to use cul-de-sac or other arrangements to allow vehicles to turn and drive forwards for most of the time. Turning arrangements should ideally be a roundabout or a 'banjo' type, although 'hammerhead' and 'stub' arrangements may be acceptable.

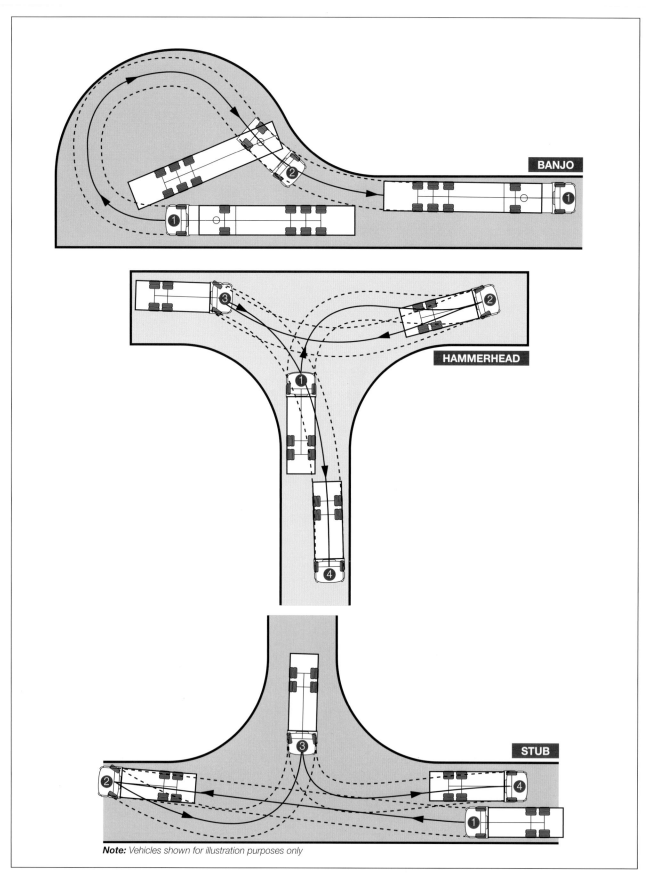

Note: Vehicles shown for illustration purposes only

Figure 7 Turning arrangements

293 If rules on vehicle movements are difficult to enforce, physical measures such as gates, barriers, flow plates (sprung flaps that only allow vehicles to cross in one direction) and control spikes (sprung tines that act the same way as flow plates, sometimes called 'crocodile teeth' or 'dragons teeth') can be very effective.

294 Forward visibility needs to be good enough to allow drivers to see and avoid hazards where appropriate. Visibility will be related to the speed that vehicles are travelling on a route, and the distance they need to avoid hazards (by stopping or changing direction safely). It will also be related to available light, environmental considerations such as dust or bad weather, the height of the driver's eyes from the road, and the general level of visibility from the vehicle.

295 There should be enough visibility at junctions and bends to allow drivers and pedestrians to see anything that might be dangerous.

296 Avoid sharp or blind bends on vehicle routes wherever possible. Where you cannot avoid them, you should consider measures such as mirrors to help drivers and pedestrians see what is around the corner.

Figure 8 Mirror to improve drivers' vision around a corner

297 A common problem is reduced visibility at junctions and bends because of landscaping. Grass banks, hedges, planters and other landscaping features can be used as traffic-calming features, but they should not interfere with drivers' and pedestrians' visibility.

298 When visibility at a bend or junction can't be improved, stop signs or signals may be appropriate. It may be necessary to prevent people from using the junction or bend altogether by enforcing a one-way system, or even blocking the road.

299 You should use road junctions and road and rail crossings as little as possible. If you have to use them, they should be clearly signed and marked to show the right of way. At rail crossings, the right of way should be in favour of trains, as even at low speeds they cannot stop easily.

300 You should think about what loads vehicles are likely to be carrying. If an accident could result in dangerous mixing of loads, or a load mixing with substances stored or piped on site, you should find a different and safe route to transport the substance wherever this is practical.

301 Vulnerable parts of the workplace (such as cast-iron columns, partitions, pipes and services) need to be protected from vehicles hitting them. The standard of protection should be based on how severe a collision could be.

302 When you are deciding how much protection a site feature needs, you need to know how likely it is that a vehicle will hit the feature, how it would hit (at what speed, from what angle, and how heavy the vehicle might be), and what the consequences would be.

303 Protective barriers should be built to the standards set out in BS 7669-3: 1994 *Vehicle restraint systems*.[9] You should read the British Standard Code of Practice BS 6180: 1999 *Barriers in and about buildings*[10] for more information.

304 Normal site features that might need protection include tanks, cylinders, silos, bund walls (which are not normally strong enough to withstand a vehicle hitting them), buildings, columns, masts, gantries and pipes.

305 By law, pedestrians or vehicles must be able to use a traffic route without causing danger to the health or safety of people working near it.

306 You need to consider protection for people who work near vehicle routes. This might involve screens to protect people who are at risk from materials that could fall from vehicles, or measures to protect people from noise or fumes.

307 Avoid using vehicles that generate potentially harmful exhaust fumes in confined spaces, where these fumes could gather and pose a health risk to drivers or others in the workplace. Adequate ventilation should always be provided. See our guide *Safe work in confined spaces*[11] for more information about using combustion engines in this sort of environment.

308 Restrict access to places where high-risk substances (for example, petrol) are stored, and where vehicles are refuelled or recharged.

309 By law, traffic routes must also keep vehicle routes far enough away from doors or gates that pedestrians use, or from pedestrian routes that lead onto them, so that the safety of pedestrians is not threatened. There needs to be enough time for a driver or a pedestrian to react successfully if they encounter one another (for example, where there is limited visibility or where other noise might mask the approach of a vehicle).

Figure 9 This well-organised building entrance separates vehicles and pedestrians as well as being clearly marked and providing signals and signs for drivers

---

Case study 5

A temporary worker was struck by a lift truck and injured as he left the site at the end of the day. As he crossed in front of a door used by lift trucks, he suffered serious injuries when the forks of an emerging vehicle knocked him down.

The employee had not heard the vehicle horn and had received no information on general workplace hazards and how to avoid them. Vehicle and pedestrian routes were not marked or segregated. There were no markings on the doors to indicate their use and drivers could not see employees outside the building, as there were no vision panels in the doors.

The site operator is responsible for assessing the risks at the workplace arising out of work activities, and for taking the measures necessary to reduce those risks so that they are as low as 'reasonably practicable'.

---

310 By law, traffic routes must also be suitably indicated where necessary, for reasons of health or safety.

311 You should mark and sign routes across open areas or yards.

312 You may also need suitable road markings and signs to alert drivers to restrictions on using traffic routes. See *Signs, signals and markings* (paragraphs 393-402) for more information.

313 You may need to highlight hazards on traffic routes by using suitable warning signs. These hazards may include:

- sharp bends;
- junctions;
- crossings;
- blind corners;
- steep gradients; and
- roadworks.

314 There is more information about pedestrian and cyclist crossing points in *Pedestrians and cyclists* in paragraphs 371-392. There is more information about hazard signs in *Signs, signals and markings* in paragraphs 393-402.

315 It may be useful to provide a plan of the workplace at the entrance (and at other appropriate points) showing vehicle routes, one-way systems and so on. This would be particularly useful at workplaces that have visiting drivers.

316 It is important to plan where certain types of vehicle operation will take place. These include loading, unloading, tipping, trimming, sheeting and other vehicle activities.

317 It is also important to plan where waste or recycling bins, skips or other containers are placed. Delivering, collecting or exchanging 'demountable' containers can need complicated and repetitive vehicle movements, and plenty of space should be allowed both around and overhead. Reversing visibility is often poor as containers block the line of sight behind the vehicle.

318 The conditions of the site should allow for any specific requirements of hook-lift or chain-lift demountables, especially in terms of the quality of the ground and the amount of overhead space needed.

Construction of traffic routes

319 The build quality of outdoor traffic routes should be similar to the standards for public highways.

320 By law, every traffic route in a workplace must be built so that the driving surface is suitable for its purpose. Also, the law requires that the surface of any traffic route must not be so uneven, potholed, sloped or slippery that any person is exposed to a risk to their health or safety.

321 Traffic routes should be maintained to provide good grip for vehicles or people. For example, they should be roughened if too smooth, gritted or sanded if slippery, and kept free of oil, grease, rubbish and other debris.

322 A surface providing extra grip may be needed on sloped driving surfaces.

323 Vehicles (including anything they are carrying) must be under a certain weight to use roads in the UK. The restriction on a vehicle's weight is linked to the number of axles it has. More weight is allowed for vehicles with more axles.

324 The maximum gross combination weight is 44 000 kg, although few vehicles operate at this weight. The more usual maximum is 38 000 kg, although vehicles with six axles and 'road-friendly' suspension can operate at 41 000 kg.

325 Traffic routes, including any bridges, ramps and other features, should be able to support the weight of the vehicles (and their loads) that are using them.

326 Structures with weight restrictions (for example, bridges) should be clearly identified.

327 Wherever possible, routes should:

■ be made of a suitable material for the location, the type of traffic, the size of the route, and the ground or foundation it is laid on;
■ have firm and even surfaces, and be properly drained; and
■ avoid steep slopes. If they are unavoidable, steep slopes should be properly signposted.

328 Steep slopes should especially be avoided in areas where lift trucks and other similar plant operate, unless they are designed to operate on slopes.

331 See *Hardstandings* (paragraphs 478-487) for more information about making sure these sorts of surface are strong enough to support the loads they need to.

332 The sort of ground or surface that the route is laid on will also make a difference to which type of paving is most suitable.

333 A surface gradient (or road camber) of about 1 in 40 should be enough to provide drainage from most areas. Run-off water should be gathered into gullies or drainage channels wherever possible, and all gratings and channel units should be strong enough to bear loads suitable to their location.

334 Connections for surface run-off from roads, hardstandings and so on may have to include 'interception facilities' where there is a risk of oil or chemical spillage.

335 You should not allow potholes to develop. If a pothole is found, it should be repaired promptly.

336 For more information on designing and maintaining driving surfaces in a way that is suitable for the vehicles that use them, see the Freight Transport Association publication *Designing for Deliveries*.[8] You can also get information from Interpave (the Precast Concrete Paving and Kerb Association) and other industry guidance.

337 You should also consider the services of a qualified engineering practice.

Surface dressing

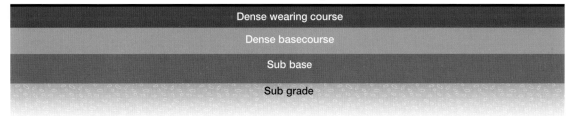

Figure 10 Diagrammatic cross section of a road

329 Suitable materials include:

■ hot rolled asphalt (or tarmac) for flexible, outdoor road-type routes;
■ concrete or another rigid material for other types of route; or
■ semi-rigid 'slab'-type constructions.

330 The type of operation that takes place on a surface should influence decisions about its design and construction. A good example is road tanker loading and unloading, where a maximum gradient of 1 in 30 is recommended to make sure the vehicle moves as little as possible, and to help contain any spillages.

Temporary workplaces and unprepared roadways

338 Temporary workplaces (for example, construction sites and forestry operations) and other types of site (for example, some farms) often have routes for vehicles and pedestrians that change as work progresses, or 'unprepared' routes such as unsurfaced roads or open ground.

339 It is important that you plan these routes carefully, including any intended changes, as they should meet the same basic safety standards that apply to 'prepared' routes. In other words, they should be suitable for their purpose, have firm and even surfaces, be properly drained, and have no slopes that are too steep.

340 Many common surfaces on temporary roadways can suffer from 'ponding' (standing water gathering). The condition of these surfaces will quickly get worse in wet conditions if they are not properly drained.

341 Try to make sure that temporary routes follow natural contours of the ground wherever possible, so that natural drainage works for you, not against you.

342 Longer sloping roads will benefit from a varying slope, rather than a constant gradient, as this will help prevent water from ponding at the bottom of the slope.

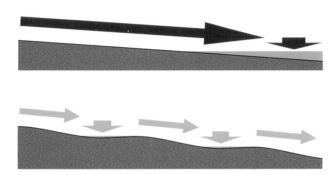

Figure 11 How a varied slope helps avoid ponding water

343 Drainage features will need to be large enough, and spaced apart, so that they can deal with the greatest expected demands on them.

344 Temporary roadways and unprepared routes can increase the risk of accidents. For example:

■ vehicles are more likely to overturn on uneven ground;
■ drivers might not be sure where to drive if there are no road markings (for example, on gravel roads); and
■ roads with poor surface friction can affect stopping distances.

345 As a result of this, you may need to place more emphasis on:

■ drivers' competence, particularly in dealing with the sorts of hazards found on unprepared routes;
■ providing information and instruction to drivers, especially if they are not familiar with the temporary roadways;
■ safe systems of work and traffic management – for example, using temporary road signs and traffic lights; and
■ supervising drivers, vehicle activities and other employees.

346 You may also need to place more emphasis on preventive checks to make sure that vehicles do not develop faults while working on unprepared roadways.

347 You may need safety banks on some routes to prevent vehicles from running over open edges, or to show a safe route.

348 We recommend that a bank should be at least 1.5 m tall or the axle height of the largest vehicle using the route (whichever is more) and be strong enough to withstand a

vehicle hitting it. Alternatively, if large rocks are used to form a safety bank, the rocks will need to be high enough and thick enough to withstand a vehicle hitting them.

349 Sometimes people have to work on public roads. These are temporary workplaces, and you can find more information about them in paragraphs 234-237.

350 See our guide *The safe use of vehicles on construction sites*[12] for workplace transport guidance that is specific to the construction industry.

Speed

351 Limiting the speed that vehicles move around the workplace is a very important part of controlling traffic.

352 The best way to do this is to use fixed features that mean drivers can't move too quickly. Examples include speed humps, narrowed routes (by bollards, raised kerbs, chicanes, built-in routeside features and so on – these are sometimes known as 'pinch points'), and 'rumble' devices (such as rumble strips, rumble areas or jiggle bars).

353 Traffic-calming measures should be signed and clearly visible. Many features can be lit or made reflective.

354 It is important to be careful when you are deciding where to use traffic-calming features, because they can sometimes actually increase risks (for example, by affecting the stability of vehicles or less secure loads).

355 Speed humps are a proven way to limit the speed that vehicles move around a traffic system. Speed humps normally slow vehicles to an average of around 15 miles per hour.

356 Warning signs should be clearly visible, and should be far enough away from the hump to allow drivers to change their speed safely. The humps themselves should also be clearly marked. See Figure 12 for an example of the type of sign you should use.

Note: Distance shown for is illustration only

Figure 12 This sign should be used to show the distance over which speed humps extend

357 For similar reasons, individual humps should not be used on their own. Humps should be repeated at intervals along a route and should not be used within 15 m of a junction or bend.

358 Speed humps are only suitable for routes where vehicles can go over the humps safely.

359 Some vehicles may not be designed to be able to go over speed humps safely (for example, most industrial lift trucks or some caravans). Also, some emergency vehicles need to avoid speed humps (for example, ambulances carrying patients with spinal injuries). However, it is often possible to include some type of bypass to allow these vehicles to avoid going over the hump.

360 Sometimes speed cushions can be used instead of speed humps. Speed cushions work in a similar way as speed humps, but do not stretch across the whole road. Instead, they leave some space clear for certain types of vehicle to drive through or straddle the raised areas (for example, cyclists or larger emergency vehicles).

Figure 13 A lift truck passing through an interrupted road hump

361 Some vehicles (for example, some lift trucks) may also have trouble passing through chicanes safely, especially if they are carrying stacked loads.

362 Speed limits are also used widely, but they need to be used sensibly. Speed limits have to be practical, otherwise drivers will be tempted to break them.

363 Common problems with speed limits are that they are poorly signed, not appropriate or not enforced. They are often set by guessing, but this can result in an unreasonable speed limit that is very difficult to enforce. Also, speedometers often don't work effectively at low speeds,

and some internal site transport vehicles don't have speedometers at all.

364 It is quite common for sites to set the same speed limit across a whole site. This is not usually effective, and can be very difficult to enforce. Often, you will need to decide on individual speed limits for different routes, because the types of traffic and task are different.

365 Speed limits need to be appropriate for:

■ the vehicles using the route;
■ the types of load they carry and how they carry them;
■ the driving surface;
■ the layout of the route, including how tight the bends are and visibility at junctions;
■ hazards along the way; and
■ work that takes place on or near the route.

366 To decide an appropriate limit, you should measure the actual speeds that vehicles are travelling at various locations along the route. The limit you decide on should be sensible considering these speeds. The limit should be a safe speed, but if it is unreasonably slow, drivers will be tempted to ignore it completely.

367 When assessing the appropriate speed limit for a particular place, you may need professional advice based on the route layout and character of the site.

368 There is more information about enforcing health and safety rules in *Control, co-operation and consultation* (paragraphs 126-153) in the chapter *Organising for safety*.

369 Speed limit signs may need to be repeated around the factory roads instead of just one sign being put up at the entrance to a limit area. This will depend on the size of the limit area, and whether drivers are likely to know (or need reminding) about the speed limit. You can find out more about how you could use signs, signals and markings in paragraphs 393-402.

Note: *Speed shown here is for illustration only*

Figure 14 Example of a maximum speed sign

370 Some systems involve controls that interact between the site and vehicles that use it. As well as information signals that sense speed and react to tell drivers that they should slow down, some systems now activate speed limiters on vehicles in response to radio signals broadcast at area boundaries.

Pedestrians and cyclists

371 Pedestrians and cyclists are very vulnerable where vehicles are being used.

372 You should provide separate routes or pavements for pedestrians to keep them away from vehicles, wherever it is reasonable to do so. Segregating pedestrians from vehicle activity, preferably by making routes entirely separate, is the most effective way of protecting them.

Figure 15 Examples of signs used to segregate pedestrians and vehicles

373 Good examples of complete segregation include footbridges (although make sure structures over traffic routes don't threaten to dislodge high loads, and consider access for disabled people) or subways.

374 Pedestrians should be kept away from areas where vehicles are working unless they need to be there. A good example of this is quarry working, where drivers are usually not allowed out of their vehicles beyond a certain point to make sure they are safe where very large surface mining vehicles are operating.

375 Where possible, pedestrian traffic routes should represent the paths people would naturally follow (often known as 'desire lines'), to encourage people to stay on them.

376 Protective barriers to keep vehicles away from pedestrian areas, and clear markings to set apart vehicle and pedestrians routes, are also effective. You can also use raised kerbs to mark vehicle and pedestrian areas.

Case study 6

A food-factory dispatch clerk was killed instantly when she was knocked down and run over by the bucket of a 15-tonne loading shovel.

Risk assessments failed to identify workplace transport issues adequately. It was regular practice for staff to walk across a warehouse where the loading shovel was operating, and no measures were put in place to prevent this.

The judge identified 'fundamental flaws of the management' and the firm was fined £400 000 following a prosecution.

Figure 16 Barrier to protect pedestrians

377 Where needed, you should provide suitable barriers or guard rails:

- at the entrances and exits to buildings;
- at the corners of buildings; and
- to prevent pedestrians from walking straight onto roads.

378 Where pedestrian and vehicle routes cross, you should provide appropriate crossing points for people to use.

379 Crossing points should be suitably marked and signposted, and should include dropped kerbs where the walkway is raised from the driving surface.

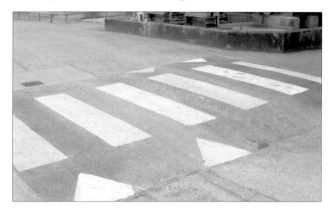

Figure 17 This pedestrian crossing has been combined with a well-marked speed hump

Figure 18 Different types of barrier

380 Where necessary, you should provide barriers or rails to prevent pedestrians from crossing at particularly dangerous points and to direct them to the crossing places. Similarly, you can use deterrent paving to guide pedestrians to the crossing points.

381 Pedestrians, cyclists and drivers should be able to see clearly in all directions at crossing points.

382 At busy crossing places, you should consider traffic lights, zebra crossings (or other types of crossing), or suitable bridges or subways as a way of segregating pedestrians from moving vehicles.

Figure 19 'Pedestrian crossing' sign

383 A standard warning sign to show a pedestrian crossing is included in *The Highway Code*.[13] It should be used in workplaces wherever appropriate. See *Signs, signals and markings* in paragraphs 393-402 for more information.

384 Where vehicle roadways are particularly wide, you may need to consider 'island' refuges to allow pedestrians and cyclists to cross the road in stages. In some cases, subways or footbridges could be necessary.

385 Where the number of vehicles, pedestrians or cyclists using a route is likely to change at regular times, you should

Figure 20 Example of a sign changing vehicle routes at certain times

consider preventing pedestrians or vehicles from using the routes at these times, to keep them apart. An example might be limiting the use of vehicles on a roadway during a shift changeover, when a lot of pedestrians are likely to be crossing.

Figure 21 Separate pedestrian and vehicle doors

386 You should provide separate vehicle and pedestrian doors wherever possible (segregation). Windows on doors can help drivers and pedestrians see whether it is safe for them to approach a door.

387 See paragraphs 258-318 in *Traffic routes* for more information about how wide routes used by pedestrians should be.

388 Routes used by vehicles inside buildings should be shown by signs and markings on the floor to tell both drivers and pedestrians.

389 On routes used by both pedestrians and automatic (driverless) vehicles, you should make sure that vehicles do not trap pedestrians. The vehicles should be fitted with safeguards to keep the risk of injury low if a vehicle hits someone. You should provide adequate clearance between the vehicles and pedestrians, and take care to make sure that fixtures along the route do not create trapping hazards.

390 There is more information about organising traffic routes to keep pedestrians safe in *Traffic routes* (see paragraphs 258-318).

391 Make sure that visiting pedestrians report to the site office, if this is appropriate. Tell visitors about site safety policies and procedures before they are allowed into areas where vehicles work.

392 In some situations, it will be appropriate to make sure that pedestrians, including any visitors, wear high-visibility clothing.

Signs, signals and markings

393 Signs are necessary to tell drivers and pedestrians about the routes they should use, and also to instruct people how to behave safely (for example, whether they must use protective equipment, and how).

Figure 22 These clear signs help arriving drivers know what to expect

394 You should use route markings to show traffic lanes, route edges, priority at junctions, stop lines, no-parking areas, pedestrian crossings and so on, and to instruct drivers (for example, 'SLOW').

395 By law, road signs used to warn or give information to traffic in private workplaces must be the same as those used on public roads, wherever a suitable sign exists. Road signs are set out in *The Highway Code*.[13] Drivers and pedestrians should be able to expect that the layout, signs, road furniture and markings on site will be similar to those on public roads.

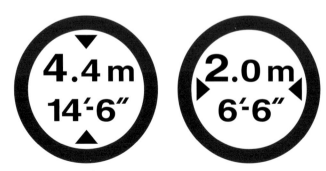

Note: Figures shown here are for illustration only

Figure 23 These signs can be used to show that no vehicles over the height or width shown can continue

396 You should use warning signs to show hazards along the way.

Note: *Sign shown here is for illustration only*

Figure 24 A sign like this should be used to show that no vehicles over a certain maximum gross weight shown can continue, and why

397 You can use traffic lights to control the flow of traffic at busy junctions, at narrow places and at site entrances. You can also use speed sensors and flashing warning signs to help control the speed of traffic.

398 You should provide signposting so that drivers do not go the wrong way. This should help prevent vehicles from moving around areas where pedestrians or other drivers might not expect them.

399 You should place signs so that people have time to see and understand them, and take any action to reduce risks before they reach the hazard.

400 All signs should:

- be clear and easy to understand;
- stand out enough to be noticed; and
- be kept clean and well maintained so that they are visible at all times.

401 If signs have to be visible in darkness, they will need to be reflective and, ideally, illuminated. Sign lighting needs be kept clean and working.

402 You can find detailed information about reflective and lit road signs in BS 873-1: 1983 *Road traffic signs and internally illuminated bollards.*[14]

Road markings

403 White road markings are used to regulate traffic, and yellow markings are used to regulate parking. Double yellow lines in particular should be applied along the edges of routes where parking is not allowed, although you should not rely on these to prevent parking in these areas without enforcement.

404 Road markings are usually applied as either a cement-based paint or as 'thermoplastic' markings. Thermoplastic markings have advantages over paint, but are slightly more expensive. Tyres can soon scrub away cement paint markings, whereas thermoplastic markings have a longer life because they grip the surface better. They also remain slightly raised for longer, making them easier to see and providing better grip for vehicles.

405 Markings are made reflective by adding tiny glass beads. These can be mixed into the marking material or dusted on the surface after it has been laid (or both).

406 Thermoplastic markings are normally both premixed and dusted with beads, but painted lines are normally only

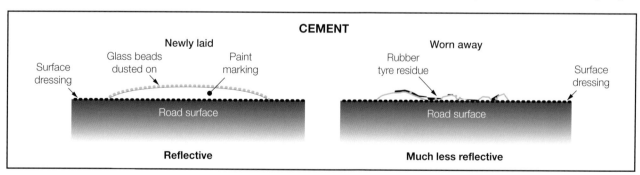

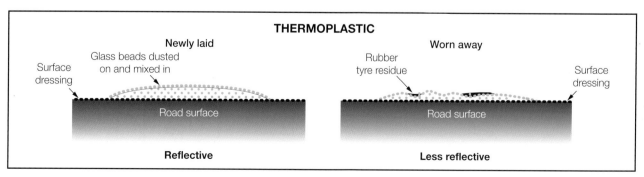

Figure 25 Road markings: when cement paint markings rub away, they become unreflective

33

dusted after they have been laid. As thermoplastic is rubbed away by vehicle tyres, more beads are exposed, but when painted lines wear away the beads are worn away, leaving the markings unreflective.

407 You should renew road markings when they fade. Markings on asphalt are laid by 'road lining' contractors, who often charge a call-out fee, so it is usually cheaper to have them lay as much as possible in one go, although this is not a reason for waiting to refresh dangerously faded markings. Your local authority highways department should be able to provide a list of these contractors in your area.

408 If the overhead clearance on a route is limited, you should consider signs to tell drivers this. If the clearance is less than 4.5 m, signs will almost certainly be needed if road vehicles might use the route. As usual, signs should be clear and easy to understand from a distance that will allow drivers to act accordingly. If possible, they should also be placed to allow drivers to choose a safe route.

Parking areas

409 Keep stationary objects, including parked vehicles, out of the flow of traffic and people around the workplace.

410 Wherever practical, you should provide parking areas for all vehicles using the workplace – that is, for work-related vehicles and for private cars, motorcycles and pedal cycles.

411 Controlled parking areas might be appropriate wherever uncontrolled parking might pose a risk to safety, for example by:

■ narrowing routes;
■ blocking sight lines; and
■ forcing pedestrians onto vehicle routes.

412 On some sites (for example, larger industrial complexes) it may be appropriate to control parking across the whole site.

Figure 26 This visitors' car park has a covered pedestrian walkway and signs telling visitors where to go

413 When drivers enter an area where parking is controlled, you should clearly tell them that they may only park in allowed places, and how they can recognise these areas. Where parking is controlled throughout the site, you should give this information at the site entrance.

414 Keep people and vehicles apart in and around parking areas by using pedestrian and vehicle exclusion areas.

Figure 27 Pedestrian walkway in car park

415 Parking areas should be in safe and suitable places.

416 If possible, drivers leaving parked vehicles should not have to cross potentially dangerous work areas or traffic routes.

417 Parking areas should:

■ be clearly signposted;
■ be firm;
■ be level;
■ be well drained;
■ not be slippery;
■ be well lit (if possible); and
■ be as close as possible to where people need to go when they leave their vehicles (for example, refreshment facilities for visiting drivers).

418 The type of parking area will depend on what vehicles are used at the workplace (including visiting vehicles), where they go and what they are used for.

419 An alternative to parking 'lots' might be bays or lay-bys, offset from the flow of traffic and people, where vehicles can be left safely. These should also be firm, level, well lit and clearly marked.

Figure 28 This fork-lift truck has been removed from the flow of traffic

420 Wherever possible, parking areas should be designed so that only simple manoeuvres are needed for vehicles to park and leave. You should always try to avoid the need for reversing, and should also think about how articulated and other large vehicles will be able to use the space safely.

421 If a driver needs to move the load area of their vehicle close to a structure, reversing will often be unavoidable. However, parking areas can often be arranged in drive-through patterns.

422 If you can't have drive-through parking, arrangements should encourage reverse parking, to reduce the number of vehicles reversing out into a flow of traffic and improve visibility for departing vehicles.

423 Arranging parking bays at an angle backwards to the flow of traffic is a good way of encouraging reverse parking.

Figure 30 Pedestrians are segregated from vehicles on this slope

425 You may need a wheel-clamping scheme (where wheel clamping is legal) or other measures to enforce parking restrictions on some sites. You should carry out these measures if somebody parks where they are not supposed to, to make sure the schemes are effective.

426 If parking is a significant problem, a full survey of parking demand and availability might be appropriate. A survey of this kind could benefit from the support of professional engineers.

427 You can find more advice about parking arrangements for cars in the Department for Transport publication *Residential Roads and Footpaths*.[15] You can find more advice about parking for larger vehicles in the Freight Transport Association guide *Designing for Deliveries*.[8]

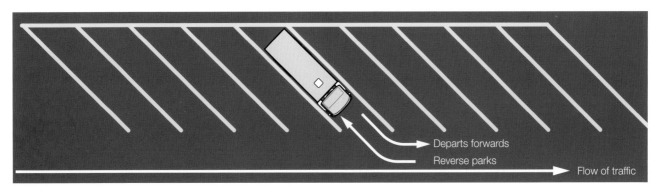

Figure 29 Parking bays angled backwards to the flow of traffic, to encourage reverse parking

424 Physical precautions such as bollards and barriers to prevent vehicles from crossing into walking areas can improve safety for pedestrians. See *Pedestrians and cyclists* (paragraphs 371-392) for more information about protecting these people.

Loading areas

428 As far as possible, loading and unloading areas should be in safe and suitable places (for example, next to marshalling areas so that vehicles can be manoeuvred easily, or near sheeting areas).

429 Wide loading areas will usually need at least two exit points, one at each end.

430 You might also consider a refuge or bolthole, to prevent people from being struck by vehicles. This could take the place of an extra pedestrian exit in a larger loading area.

Case study 7

A joiner suffered severe head injuries when he fell from the top of a stack of timber on the back of a flatbed lorry.

The joiner was helping to unload the delivery when he climbed on top of a timber stack. While edging along the stack, he lost his footing and fell. An unloading bay with a concrete platform was available to provide safe access for unloading vehicles, but was not used.

The joiner should have received training and instruction on how to unload safely, using the unloading bay. Supervision should have ensured that he followed those instructions. Because instruction was not provided, the joiner should have waited in a safe area until unloading had finished. Climbing on top of loads should be avoided whenever 'reasonably practicable'.

---

431 Loading areas are often arranged into bays, with a raised platform for vehicles to park against that allows site staff to move straight into the load body.

432 Designers will try to fit as many bays as possible into an area, to allow for the largest possible number of vehicles to be loaded or unloaded at one time. However, it is important that there is enough space around bays for vehicles to move safely into and out of the bay, and for people to move around the vehicle without being trapped.

433 The height of vehicle load platforms can vary quite a lot – even between when a single vehicle is empty or loaded. This can mean that the difference in height between the loading bay platform and the vehicle load platform varies. Loading and unloading workers need to be aware of this. It is better to have a bay platform slightly lower than the vehicle platform, rather than one that is slightly higher.

434 'Dock levellers' (adjustable ramps that can cover the height difference between the vehicle and bay platforms) are common. They should not be extended to a steep slope either downwards or upwards, because this can mean that anything crossing the surface is difficult to control.

435 Many dock levellers use a hinged lip to connect the ramp to the vehicle load platform. Care should be taken that this lip does not trap anything as it is unfolds or folds. People using this equipment should be competent to do so safely.

Figure 31 An extended dock leveller linking a loading bay to a vehicle load body

436 Visibility during reversing is always important, and especially where pedestrians may have no escape route from a vehicle approaching them.

437 In particular, where articulated vehicles have to reverse-steer into an area, visibility to the back of the vehicle is often blocked by parts of the trailer (you should recognise this during risk assessments). A system of work telling the driver whether it is safe to reverse may be appropriate.

438 The edges of loading bays need to be marked clearly.

439 Where there is a danger of people falling off platforms or bays in loading areas, the platforms or bays may need to be fenced – for example, by secure guard rails (designed so that goods can be passed safely over or under them, or removable sections of railing may be used if this is properly supervised). If fencing is not practical, other safeguards may be needed.

440 You may also need to provide protection against bad weather. For example, strong winds can be very dangerous during loading. See chapters *Loading and unloading, and load safety* and *Preventing falls from workplace vehicles* for more information about loading conditions and practices, and preventing falls from vehicles.

441 Dock shelters and dock houses can help to control loading and unloading conditions. In these arrangements, a vehicle reverses directly up to an opening in the side of the building, where a weather seal is created around the opened end of the vehicle.

442 You should take care that these shelters do not create their own trapping or machinery hazards. People using this equipment should be competent to do so safely. Anything that creates a seal around the back of a goods vehicle can also reduce the amount of communication that takes place between the delivery driver and site workers, which can introduce additional risk. This should be recognised in your risk assessment.

443 There is a risk that static electricity can build up where flowing solids are released through a hose or a chute. Delivery workers could receive an electric shock, or sparks from this electrical charge could start a fire or an explosion (for example, in a cloud of dust or fumes). You may need to provide earthing points to allow this charge to escape to earth safely through vehicle-mounted equipment.

444 You can find more advice about loading bay arrangements and loading areas in general in the Freight Transport Association guide *Designing for Deliveries*.[8]

Site-based ways to stop vehicles from moving

445 Preventing vehicles from moving during loading and unloading operations can be important to make sure that people who might be working on or around the vehicle are protected.

446 Preventing vehicles from moving until it is safe to do so is also important to reduce the risk of leaks, spillages or falling loads, especially where dangerous loads are being transferred.

447 You may need to think about ways to prevent drivers from leaving too early – this is known as a 'driveaway' accident. Driveaways can have very serious consequences, especially if lift trucks are involved.

448 Measures could include:

- vehicle or trailer restraints;
- traffic lights, barriers or other 'stop'-type signals;
- various systems for controlling access to vehicle keys or the cab; and
- safe systems of work that make sure the driver is aware of when it is safe to leave.

449 Vehicles can also 'creep' away from the edge of the loading bay as machines handling the materials jolt the vehicle when they move between the bay platform and the vehicle. This can cause a large gap, or can lead to a ramp suddenly slipping from the vehicle, causing vehicles or people to fall.

450 Systems to prevent vehicles from moving can either be built into the design of the vehicle or be site based.

451 This section deals with the methods that remain in one workplace and deal with different vehicles as they pass through. The advantage of these systems is that they are directly under the control of the site.

452 See *Vehicle-based ways to stop vehicles from moving* (paragraphs 575-591) for more information about vehicle-based methods. While vehicle-based methods can be very effective, relying on them assumes that they are checked and maintained by the vehicle operators. This places them out of the direct control of the site operator. As a result, site operators often need to take their own precautions.

453 Systems that rely on people's actions are less reliable than engineered solutions.

Figure 32 This concrete wheel stop helps make sure vehicles do not drive into a pedestrian area

454 The simplest way to prevent a vehicle from moving is to place chocks (large wedges of hard material) beneath the wheels. The chocks will resist movement, and should be at least large enough to be noticed by a driver trying to move with them in place. They should also be brightly coloured, to make them visible to drivers and other workers.

455 Chocks should always be removed when it is time for the vehicle to move away. A safe system of work covering the use of wheel chocks is very important, as workers who put them in place or remove them will be in a dangerous place. Drivers should know not to move until they have been signalled that it is safe to do so by a designated person, who should be sure workers are in a safe place before allowing movement. It may be necessary to halt vehicle movements (such as delivery vehicles arriving in adjacent bays) while chocks are being put in place or removed.

456 You can use other methods to restrain the vehicle. Some systems clamp to a part of the vehicle, such as the rear under-run bar. However, larger vehicles are often very powerful, and sometimes simply rip restraint devices from their moorings when they begin to move. Other methods are like advanced versions of chocks that are fixed to the floor of the loading bay.

457 Some methods force drivers to apply the semi-trailer emergency brakes before they can unlock the gate of the dock shelter. These are effective at preventing driveaways, but you should be careful that you do not encourage drivers

to rely on emergency brakes as a way of keeping a semi-trailer stationary – parking brakes should also be applied.

458 Signals such as traffic lights can be effective, although they do not actually prevent a vehicle from moving without some sort of barrier or safe system of work as well.

Figure 33 A well-organised loading bay, using traffic lights to inform drivers, and using visibility marking effectively

459 A relatively cost-effective way of placing a barrier in front of a vehicle is to arrange a stop sign (which is tall enough to be seen from the vehicle cab) in a palletised concrete block. Site staff with lifting equipment (for example, a lift truck) can place this in front of the vehicle and then remove it when it is safe for the vehicle to leave. It is very important that a safe system of work is followed to make sure that anyone moving around in vehicle marshalling areas is kept safe.

460 Applying the handbrake and removing the keys are standard measures to make sure a vehicle can't be driven away too early.

461 You should consider removing the vehicle keys or paperwork, and keeping them away from the driver. Systems like this (sometimes called 'key-safe' or 'custody' systems) usually cost very little and are widely used, often in support of traffic light systems. If you use a key-safe system,

the keys should be kept out of reach until it is safe for the vehicle to be moved. A good way of achieving this is by placing them on a hook attached to the back of a loading bay door, where this is possible.

Figure 34 These hooks keep keys away from the vehicles until loading has been completed

462 However, many drivers now carry extra keys, as they prefer to remain in control of their vehicle. As a result, some sites do not allow drivers to stay in the vehicle during loading and unloading.

463 Although this is a good way of preventing driveaway accidents, you should consider the welfare of the driver. Drivers may have sleeping space or other facilities in their cab. Their welfare and safety, and that of other site and road users, might be better protected by finding an alternative that is as effective at preventing driveaways, especially where drivers may be stopping between long journeys.

464 If drivers are not allowed in their vehicles, it is important that you provide them with a safe area to wait that allows them to rest effectively between driving shifts, especially where they may be waiting for several hours.

465 Although by law everyone involved in loading a vehicle is responsible for the vehicle being loaded safely, goods drivers in particular need to make sure that their vehicle has been well loaded, because they drive on public roads.

466 Where drivers need to observe the loading, they will need to be in a safe place to do this. This should be away from danger (for example away from moving vehicles, or places where loads could fall) and should be a clearly marked.

467 Even where drivers carry extra sets of keys, key-safe systems can help make sure that site workers and visiting drivers communicate about when it is safe to drive away.

468 These safeguards would be especially effective where there may be communication problems (for example, where drivers who do not speak English are involved).

469 Ignition controls (such as keys or fobs) should not be left in the vehicles when they are parked.

Weighbridges

470 Weighbridges often mark the point beyond which visiting drivers are not allowed to leave their vehicles. This is a good way of separating visiting pedestrians from dangerous vehicle movements (segregation).

471 In older factories, the weighbridge was often placed just inside the factory gate so that vehicles entering or leaving the site could use it.

472 When site entrances hosting weighbridges are also used by other traffic, they can block the flow of traffic.

473 Where possible, weighbridges should be placed so that they do not block traffic flow.

474 Visiting drivers may also need space away from the traffic flow after they have crossed the weighbridge, to park up and check, trim and sheet their load in safety, before leaving the site. See *Site-based access to vehicles* (paragraphs 498-522) and chapter *Trimming, sheeting and netting* for more information on providing facilities to help people do these tasks safely. These areas should be able to handle the number of vehicles that need to use them.

475 The consequences of a vehicle tipping over the side of a weighbridge can be very severe, and could be even worse if the weighbridge is 'elevated' (higher than the normal driving surface). The people at risk are the driver and anyone else in, on or around the vehicle.

476 If there are buildings close to the weighbridge, the people in the buildings could also be at risk if a vehicle falls on the building – especially if the building is fragile.

477 You need to take measures to prevent vehicles from falling over. Edges of roads, loading platforms etc should be clearly marked, and prevention features that are strong enough to withstand the force of a falling vehicle might be appropriate. Measures to help drivers line their vehicles up properly should also help prevent vehicles from being driven over the edge.

Hardstandings

478 Places where vehicles and their trailers park up for any reason should be 'hardstanding'.

479 This means they should be strong enough to safely support the weight of the vehicle, trailer and load as it rests on the surface (through the wheels and any outriggers or other stabilisers).

480 They should also be able to withstand the corrosive effect of any spilled loads, fuel, oil and other pollutants without being made significantly weaker.

481 If a vehicle parks up or tries any other operation (for example, tipping) on an area that cannot support it, it may overbalance if the ground underneath gives way.

482 Cement concrete surfaces are normally better than asphalt or bituminous surfaces where goods vehicles stand to load or unload, because they are often better at supporting heavy loads over a small area.

483 Also, asphalt or bitumen used as a binder in surface coatings is not usually resistant to spilled or leaked oil, petrol or some other chemicals.

484 If you use bituminous surfaces, you are likely to need padding (sometimes known as 'load-spreading plates') under semi-trailer landing legs because these surfaces are less able to support heavy loads over a small area.

485 However, this sort of padding is not always effective. This is because for the plates to be strong enough to be useful, they often need to be very heavy.

486 Drivers should be aware that a prepared surface can look much the same from above, no matter how well it is constructed. A surface may look strong enough but may not be suitably hardstanding.

487 Drivers should check with informed site workers if they are in doubt. It is important that site workers are able to accurately tell them where it is safe for them to park up.

Lighting

488 By law, every workplace must have suitable and sufficient lighting.

489 All roads, manoeuvring areas and yards should be adequately lit. Areas near junctions, buildings, plant, pedestrian routes and areas, and places where vehicles or mobile plant regularly move, all need particular attention.

490 You can find more advice about indoor lighting in the *Code for Lighting*[16] published by the Society of Light and Lighting and the Chartered Institute of Building Services Engineers. Our publication *Lighting at work* HSG38[17] also provides information and guidance for lighting workplaces.

491 Where lights are placed can be very important.

492 Tall vehicles can block light, even when it comes from windows or lamps that are placed high on posts, or on walls, ceilings, canopies and so on. Lights should be placed over the space between vehicle bays, rather than over the centre of the bay where they will be blocked by a tall vehicle.

493 If drivers have to reverse towards strong lights, you should make sure that the lights are not placed or angled so that they dazzle the driver either directly or in their mirrors.

494 Places where work is carried out around moving vehicles should be very well lit (for example, with floodlights) where work happens during the hours of darkness.

495 Lighting must not be a nuisance to the local environment, so this might influence where you put the lighting and how strong it is. You can get advice about this from your local authority Environmental Health department.

496 Glare from the sun can sometimes be a problem for drivers, so you may need measures to avoid this (for example, sun visors).

497 You may also need measures to avoid sudden changes in lighting levels – for example, when moving from a dark warehouse to a bright day, or from a dark night to a strongly lit building. Moving too quickly from bright to darker areas (and from dark to brighter areas) makes it hard to see, and can make closed-circuit television (CCTV) systems much less effective, as they can take time to adjust to different lighting levels. Our guide *Lighting at work*[17] provides more guidance about how to arrange lighting to allow for the change between differently lit areas.

Site-based access to vehicles

498 Vehicle activities that mean workers need access to different parts of vehicles are quite common. Apart from loading and unloading, workers may need access to parts of vehicles in order to clean them, trim aggregate loads and manually sheet loads, and so on.

499 This section deals with the site-based structures used for accessing parts of different vehicles as they pass through the site. The advantage of these structures is that they are directly under the control of the site.

500 The main types of structure are platforms and gantries.

501 Most platforms are simple drive-through or drive-past structures. Although designs with three fixed sides are sometimes used, they should be avoided, as vehicles need to reverse to use them.

502 If a three-sided structure is going to be used, you can avoid the need for reversing by making the end platform moveable. The vehicle can drive in forwards between the two fixed side platforms, and then the end platform can be replaced and secured behind the vehicle. As with other mobile work platforms, these should only be used once a competent person has checked it is safe to do so.

503 Drivers need to be able to pull up very closely alongside the platform to prevent falls between the side of the vehicle and the edge of the platform.

504 Platforms do have some disadvantages:

■ if workers need access to vehicles of different sizes, platforms may be a problem because they are usually a fixed height, so cannot be changed to match the heights of different vehicles;
■ drive-through platforms are also usually a fixed width and so can't be made to match the widths of different vehicles.

505 Gantries can be more suitable where lots of different sized vehicles are expected, because they are useful for a wider range of vehicle sizes.

506 A gantry would normally be a small platform with an overhead beam reaching over the vehicle. A harness system is attached to the beam. The worker will stand on the load

or vehicle, but the system will help prevent the danger of the worker falling a long way. The system is likely to be either of the 'work-restraint' type (which will prevent the worker from approaching a dangerous area like the edge of the vehicle), or the 'fall-arrest' type (which does not prevent a fall, but will make it less serious).

507 Both the gantry structure and the harness system need to be strong enough to take the worker's weight in case they fall.

508 However, gantries do rely on a safe system of work being used, as drivers need to be trained to use harness systems properly. If this is 'one-off' work, the worker will need to be supervised while using the equipment.

509 There need to be enough platforms or gantries to allow for the largest number of vehicles likely to need them at one time. Drivers might choose to bypass the system to avoid queuing if there are not enough spaces.

510 Platforms and walking surfaces on gantry structures should be level, stable and strong, and should provide good walking grip. Both types of structure should be clearly marked to help prevent vehicles from striking them.

511 Platforms or gantries should not be used if weather conditions are bad enough to threaten safety of workers.

512 Platforms and gantries should have a safe way for people to get onto them and down from them. You should consider in advance how any worker who has suffered a fall can be rescued.

513 Stairs can be much more effective than ladders if workers are likely to be carrying something (such as a bag, toolbox, or tools).

514 Steps should be made of slip-resistant grating or another slip-resistant material with enough space for mud or oil to pass through the grate and away from the walking surface.

515 Rungs or steps should be level and give plenty of toehold or foothold. Rounded rungs are the least safe, as they become slippery easily and can be uncomfortable to use.

516 Steps, stairs and ladders should have sound hand and guard rails that are co-ordinated with the footholds, and the lower part should be easily reached from wherever workers are using them. Handrails are better than individual handholds, as they can be used without the worker having to remove their hand from the rail.

517 Some platforms are only meant to help drivers get onto or down from a vehicle.

518 This helps reduce the distance a person is likely to fall, because they land on the platform instead of the ground, which makes it less likely that a person will be seriously injured. They also make falls less likely, because a person does not have to climb around as much.

519 Platforms benefit from well-constructed and suitably high barriers around them, to prevent people from falling off. It may be suitable to have several rails, to protect people who work when crouched or standing. This is obviously not practical if the driver needs to get onto the vehicle itself.

520 You can also use platforms and gantries to improve safety during load trimming. See chapter *Trimming, sheeting and netting* for more information on trimming loads safely.

521 In some workplaces (for example, landfill sites) gantries and platforms may need to be moved around. They should be used only after a competent person has checked it is safe to do so.

522 If there is any doubt as to whether a platform or gantry is suitable to be used, it should not be used.

Housekeeping

523 If vehicles or other obstructions are left blocking traffic ways, or if driving or walking surfaces become littered, slippery or too dirty, they may cause significant risks to health and safety.

524 By law, traffic routes must, so far as is 'reasonably practicable', be kept free from obstructions and from anything that may cause a person to slip, trip or fall.

525 By law, every floor in a workplace, and the surface of every traffic route, must be kept free from obstructions, so far as is 'reasonably practicable'.

526 For more about what 'reasonably practicable' means, see paragraphs 35-50.

527 Spilled loads, or anything that falls from a vehicle or anywhere else that could be a danger, should be removed or cleaned up as soon as possible.

528 Site operators should make sure that waste containers are available:

- wherever used packaging or other refuse is likely to gather;
- are big enough; and
- are suitable for their intended use.

529 Wherever it is practical, site operators should make sure that there are specified places for moveable objects, and that whenever they are being left overnight or for long periods of time, they are kept in their proper place.

Maintenance areas

530 Where maintenance work has to be carried out on or near roads, vehicle traffic should be kept away from those doing the work. This may involve using cones or barriers, or closing the route to vehicles.

Safe vehicles

Safe vehicles in general

531 By law, every employer must make sure that work equipment (which includes vehicles) is suitable for its purpose.

532 The law also requires that every employer, when choosing work equipment, must take account of the working conditions and the risks to the health and safety of people using the work equipment.

533 By law, employers must also take account of any further risk posed by the use of chosen work equipment.

534 The design of vehicles used on public roads has to meet specific legal standards, set out in the Road Vehicles (Construction and Use) Regulations. The overall standard of vehicles used in workplaces should be at least as good as for public roads. In some cases, there are specific supply standards dealing with mobile plant in the workplace (for example, some lift trucks).

535 Some workplaces or types of work are particularly dangerous (for example, building sites), so there may need to be specific standards for vehicles used in these places.

Suitable for the task

536 Workplace vehicles should be stable under working conditions and provide a safe way to get into and out of the cab, and any other parts of the vehicle that need to be accessed regularly.

537 Access features on vehicles, such as ladders, steps or walkways, should have the same basic features as site-based access systems. See chapter *Preventing falls from workplace vehicles* and *Site-based access to vehicles* (paragraphs 498-522) for more information on safe ways of accessing vehicles.

Case study 8

An employee of a logistics firm was delivering to a distribution warehouse in a curtain-sided lorry, when he received a serious hand injury.

A warehouse employee was using a fork-lift truck to offload pallets of newspapers. The trailer's centre pole was obstructing one of the pallets. The lorry driver tried to remove the pole manually, but other pallets were pushing against it so he couldn't remove the locking pin. It was decided to relieve pressure on the locking pin by using the fork-lift truck to push the pole, and the lorry driver's hand was either struck or trapped by one of the forks, which severed his index finger.

The firms' risk assessments had failed to identify this unsafe system of work, which was common practice in the warehouse. Both firms were prosecuted and have now revised their systems and trained staff how to remove poles safely.

538 It is important that drivers are able to see clearly around their vehicle, to allow them to spot hazards and avoid them. See *Visibility from vehicles and reversing aids* (paragraphs 550-570) for more information.

539 You should consider fitting a horn, vehicle lights, reflectors, reversing lights and possibly other warning devices (for example, rotating beacons or reversing alarms). See *Visibility from vehicles and reversing aids* (paragraphs 550-570) for more information.

540 You should use suitable painting and markings to make the vehicle stand out.

541 Vehicles should have seats and seat belts (or other restraints where necessary) that are safe and comfortable.

542 There need to be guards on dangerous parts of the vehicle (for example, power take-offs, chain drives, exposed hot exhaust pipes).

543 Vehicles should be suitable for any loads carried, and it is especially important that the vehicle has adequate anchor points to make sure that loads can be carried securely.

Figure 35 Well-marked yard shunter

544 If loads are secured to the vehicle, the places where the load straps are attached (anchored) to the vehicle need to be strong enough to take the strain. The Department for Transport guide *Safety of Loads on Vehicles*[18] gives detailed advice about vehicles carrying loads on public roads, much of which is relevant to securing loads to workplace vehicles. When securing loads:

■ anchor points should be designed so that they spread the weight and forces they receive into the main structure of the vehicle;

■ if an anchor point has moving parts, they should move as little as possible when loaded by a restraint, as any movement will seriously reduce how effective the restraint is;

■ the anchor points must be compatible with the type of securing equipment likely to be used;

■ we recommend that the attachments meet the relevant British Standards (for example, eye bolts to BS 4278[19] and shackles to BS 3551);[20]

■ anchor points should be firmly attached either directly to the chassis or to a metal crosspiece or outrigger;

■ anchor points that are secured only to wooden members are unlikely to be strong enough;

■ if anchor points are fixed at or in the area that will be loaded (for example, the load platform of a flat-bed lorry), they should not stick out above the level of the loading area when they are not being used (for example, they could sit in a dedicated niche);

■ the size of any niche should be no larger than is necessary for the particular anchorage used.

545 When individual parts need to be replaced because of wear or damage, load-retention strapping, demountable lifting chains, lifting cables and other systems should be replaced in sets wherever this is reasonable. This helps to make sure that there are not large differences in the levels of stress that different pieces have been exposed to.

546 Vehicles should provide protection for drivers from bad weather, or an inhospitable working environment (for example, very high or low temperatures, dirt, dust, fumes, or excessive noise or vibration).

547 Drivers have been known to fix materials across overhead parts of a vehicle (such as the falling-object protection on a lift truck) to provide some shelter from the weather. This is a sign that properly engineered weather protection is probably necessary.

548 No one should be allowed to climb around parts of vehicles that are not designed to support them, and no one should act in a way that could result in slipping and accidentally activating vehicle controls.

Case study 9

An employee received fatal injuries when he was crushed between the mast and the top of the overhead guard of an industrial counterbalance lift truck.

He accidentally operated the mast tilt with his boot as he climbed onto the dashboard to wrap plastic film over the overhead structure to protect himself from heavy rain. The lift truck engine had been left on and handbrake off.

Although eight lift truck drivers worked for the firm, several had not had refresher training for many years, and two had received no training at all. The use of cling film for weather protection was common, as was the fitting of wood or metal covers on lift trucks.

The truck was mainly used outside, but the company had not assessed the need for a cover. Appropriate weatherproofing should have been fitted; access to the bulkhead should have been restricted and accidental use of the controls prevented by fitting a transparent half-screen.

The firm was prosecuted and fined £5000 with £3000 costs.

---

549 Where appropriate, vehicles should have driver protection to prevent injury if the vehicle overturns, and to prevent the driver from being hit by falling objects. This could include roll protection, operator restraints and falling-object protection. See chapter *Preventing vehicles from overturning* for further information about roll-over protection and driver restraints.

Visibility from vehicles and reversing aids

550 Vehicles should have large enough windscreens (with wipers where necessary) and external mirrors to provide adequate all-round visibility.

Figure 36 Side-mounted mirrors

551 Road-going vehicles are fitted with conventional side mirrors, and it is often worthwhile adding extra mirrors to reduce blind spots for drivers.

Figure 37 Mirrors fitted to off-highway construction plant

552 Side mirrors angled to allow drivers of larger vehicles to see cyclists and pedestrians alongside their vehicles are also available, and can be effective in improving visibility around the vehicle from the driving position. These mirrors are fitted to larger road-going vehicles as standard.

553 Items should not be placed in the windscreen area or in the way of mirrors or monitors, where they might get in the way of visibility from the driving position. A good guide can be that the area of the windscreen that is kept clear by the wipers should not be obscured, and nor should the side windows.

554 Windows and mirrors will also normally need to be kept clean and in good repair. Dirt or cracks can make windows or mirrors less effective.

555 Vehicle windows in some workplaces may need to be made of a material that can resist objects flying towards them (for example, where drivers are at risk from broken chainsaw blades during forestry operations).

556 Some types of vehicle (such as straddle carriers, large shovel loaders and some large quarry vehicles) often have poor visibility from the cab. Visibility can be poor to the side or front of a vehicle as well as behind, and loads on vehicles can severely limit the visibility from the driving position.

557 Lift trucks and compact dumper vehicles in particular can have difficulty with forward visibility when they are transporting bulky loads. You should recognise the risks associated with this reduced visibility in your risk assessment. For more information on doing your transport risk assessment, see *Managing the risks*.

558 Closed-circuit television (CCTV) may be appropriate for some vehicles where the driver can't see clearly behind or around the vehicle.

Figure 38 CCTV monitor in vehicle cab

559 CCTV can cover most blind spots. The cost of fitting CCTV systems has fallen since the technology was first developed, and the systems are also more reliable. The cost of fitting a system to a vehicle varies with the type of camera, link and monitor. Companies who have fitted CCTV have found that it can reduce the number of reversing accidents, and in this way the systems usually pay for themselves in a few years.

560 Both black-and-white and colour systems are available. Colour systems can provide a clearer image where there is little contrast (for example, outside on an overcast day). However, black-and-white systems normally provide a better image in lower light or darkness, and usually come with infrared systems, which can be more effective than standard cameras where work happens outside during the hours of darkness.

561 Monitors should have adjustable contrast, brightness and resolution controls to make them useful in the different light conditions in which they are likely to be used. It may be necessary to shield any monitor from glare by using a hood.

562 If possible, the camera for a CCTV system should be fitted in a high position in the middle of the vehicle's rear where one camera is being used, or in the upper corners where two cameras are used. This will provide a better angle for the driver to judge distance and provide a greater field of vision. It also keeps the camera clear of a lot of the dust and spray that can make cameras less effective, as well as usually being out of the reach of thieves or vandals.

563 However, CCTV systems do have the following limitations:

■ if vehicles are leaving a darker area to a more strongly lit area (for example, driving out of a building), the change in the level of brightness can mean that CCTV systems do not work for a moment as they adjust;
■ a dirty lens will make a camera much less effective;
■ it can be difficult for drivers to judge heights and distances on CCTV monitors.

564 It is important that using CCTV systems does not lead to drivers being complacent about safety. Operators need to know how to use the equipment properly, and should be trained in using CCTV systems.

Figure 39 High centre-mounted CCTV camera

565 Other types of system to improve awareness for both pedestrians and drivers are available.

566 Alarms such as radar and other devices that sense nearby obstructions are increasingly being fitted to road-going vehicles as parking aids.

567 These systems may be useful as reversing aids on open sites where the number of unwanted alarms is likely to be low. Sensing alarms may not be as effective where they would be set off very often. Their range is usually limited to about 2 m.

568 Reversing alarms can be fitted. They should be kept in working order. The alarm should be loud and distinct enough to make sure that it does not become part of the background noise.

569 Reversing alarms are sometimes not useful as they may be drowned out by other noise, or may be so common on a busy site that pedestrians do not take any notice. It can also be hard to know exactly where an alarm is coming from, and people who are less able to hear are also at greater risk. Alarms can also disturb nearby residents.

570 Using reversing alarms may be appropriate (based on your risk assessment) but might be most effectively used along with further measures to reduce risks that result from reversing vehicles, such as warning lights.

Manoeuvrability

571 Accidents often happen because people become trapped or crushed by part of a rear-wheel steer or tracked vehicle (like the counterbalance on a lift truck) that they were not expecting to move in a certain way.

572 As part of your workplace transport risk assessment, it is important that you understand the handling characteristics of the vehicles that use your site.

573 You should use this knowledge to help you make decisions about the layout of your site, and how you can make sure that people are safe. See *Traffic routes* (paragraphs 258-318) for more information on designing routes that are able to accommodate the vehicles and pedestrians using them.

574 It may be appropriate for you to make sure that people know about the way different types of vehicle move before they are allowed into an area where vehicles operate.

Vehicle-based ways to stop vehicles from moving

575 It is important to make sure that vehicles do not move when they are parked (and during loading, unloading and other operations) so that people who might be working on or around the vehicle are protected.

576 Systems to prevent vehicles from moving can either be built into the design of the vehicle or be site based. For more information about site-based systems, see *Site-based ways to stop vehicles from moving* (paragraphs 445-469).

577 Vehicles should have suitable and effective brakes, both for general service and for parking.

578 Some tanker vehicles have a safety system that prevents the vehicle brakes from being released until the delivery hose has been stored. These systems prevent the tanker from driving away while the delivery is still underway. This is an effective engineered solution, but workers should not use a site-based hose instead of these systems, leaving the vehicle hose stored and the safety system inactive.

579 On some vehicles, the handbrake is designed to secure the rear wheels only. Fully extending the outriggers on some vehicles may raise the rear wheels off the ground, which might mean that the handbrake does not work.

580 Consider fitting four-wheel braking systems or other effective methods to make sure the vehicle cannot move during loading.

581 If it is reasonable, fit outriggers with plates instead of wheels, to increase contact with the ground.

582 If manufacturers provide wheel chocks, use these at all times when vehicles are stationary. Information on chocking should be provided with the vehicle operating instructions.

583 You should instruct drivers to make sure that the wheels remain in contact with the ground when operating outriggers, and to use chocks where provided.

584 The 'fail-safe' type of emergency air brakes on semi-trailers lock the trailer wheels when the air hose connection with the trailer (the 'suzie') is disconnected. This is so that if the trailer breaks away from the tractive unit (for example, in a crash), the line is broken and the brakes are applied to stop the trailer.

585 Drivers sometimes use the emergency brakes as parking brakes when they uncouple the tractive and semi-trailer units, because they have to disconnect the suzie anyway. This should never be allowed to happen. Air brakes should never be applied solely by disconnecting the suzie hose. The emergency brakes should not be relied on to secure a semi-trailer.

586 Although the actual brakes on this sort of system are the same for both the parking and emergency brakes, the control mechanism is very different, and emergency brakes should never be relied on to secure a semi-trailer.

587 Reconnecting the hose will free the brakes immediately, leaving the vehicle free to move with the driver away from the cab. These accidents are called 'vehicle runaways' and can mostly be prevented.

588 When vehicle runaway accidents happen, they often cause very serious injuries because there are usually people around the vehicle (for example, the driver). Even if nobody is hurt, there is likely to be significant and expensive damage to the vehicle, buildings or other plant.

589 Making sure that both the tractive unit and semi-trailer parking brake controls are used is the most effective way of making vehicle runaways less likely.

590 Alarm systems that go off if the driver tries to leave the vehicle cab without applying the handbrake are now available. These systems may help to make vehicle runaway accidents less likely where tractive units fitted with these alarms are involved. However, they will not help make sure that semi-trailer parking brakes have been applied, and so are not a complete solution to the problem of vehicle runaways.

591 Relying on the tractive unit handbrake to secure a semi-trailer is not safe. These brakes are not designed to hold the combined weight of the tractive unit and a semi-trailer. Also, a different tractive unit might be involved, and it may not be fitted with the same sort of alarm system.

Skips, containers and demountables

592 A range of 'demountable' containers (such as chain-lift skips, hook-lift containers, compactors and 'twist-lock' shipping containers) are used in industry. They vary greatly in size and condition.

593 Serious and fatal accidents have been caused by poor maintenance or the failure of door locks, or failure of the parts that secure demountables to vehicles.

594 'Jogging' is where drivers reverse and brake hard to free blocked material from skips. Avoid this because it can lead to too much wear to the parts securing the containers, leading to their failure and the uncontrolled release of the container itself.

595 You can find more information on risks during tipping, some design considerations and suggestions for safe systems of work in chapter *Tipping*.

596 You should instruct and train drivers and operators to regularly inspect bins, doors and restraining devices and to report faults.

597 You must check that faults are put right and provide a maintenance system for skips and containers. Keep a record of the checks carried out and any resulting action.

598 Several fatal accidents have involved skip or bulk loader runaways during loading or tipping activities.

599 Accidents have happened where the twist-lock fixings which secure shipping containers to transporters have not been properly released before trying to lift the container clear of the vehicle. This can result in the vehicle being lifted with the container, and can be very dangerous.

600 Lifting-machinery operators should not begin to move containers until ground workers have confirmed that all of the locks have been released. Ground workers should not provide this signal until they are confident that it is correct.

Maintenance, repair and retrofitting

601 By law, every employer must make sure that work equipment is maintained in an efficient state, in efficient working order and in good repair.

602 Our publication *Health and safety in motor vehicle repair*[21] provides guidance on safe working practices for maintaining motor vehicles.

603 It is important that vehicles are maintained so that they are mechanically in good condition.

Case study 10

A shunt driver fell from a lorry cab because of a faulty door. He hit his head on a concrete floor at his company's depot and died some days later from his injuries.

The company had failed to deal with the faulty handle because of a 'systemic failure' in the company's vehicle checks. The shunt vehicles were treated as low priority for repairs and maintenance, and vehicle servicing was often late.

The company was fined £150 000 and ordered to pay £21 000 in costs. Since the accident, new vehicles have been bought and maintenance improved.

604 Inspections could range from drivers carrying out start-up safety checks before using the vehicle (such as checking that the tyres are properly inflated) to regular preventive maintenance inspections carried out based on time or mileage. Each vehicle you purchase or hire should come with a handbook giving manufacturer's guidance on regular maintenance.

605 To help identify problems which may happen while the vehicle is being used, the driver will need instruction or training on carrying out appropriate checks and reporting any problems.

606 Employers may find it helpful to give drivers a list of daily checks to sign off for their vehicles.

607 Planned maintenance is also needed to help prevent failures during use.

608 Planned maintenance should be thorough, regular and frequent enough to meet the manufacturer's guidelines and common sense. You should pay special attention to:

- the braking system;
- the steering system;
- the tyres;
- mirrors and any fittings that allow the driver to see clearly (for example, CCTV cameras);
- the windscreen washers and wipers;
- any warning devices (for example, horns, reversing alarms or lights);

- any ladders, steps, walkways or other parts that support people or make it easier for them to access parts of the vehicle;
- any pipes, pneumatic or hydraulic hoses, rams, outriggers, lifting systems or other moving parts or systems; and
- any specific safety systems (for example, control interlocks to prevent the vehicle or its equipment from moving unintentionally), racking, securing points for ropes and so on.

609 Wherever relevant, the following precautions should be taken when maintaining vehicles:

- brakes should be applied and, where necessary, wheels should be chocked;
- engines should always be started and run with brakes on and in neutral gear;
- raised parts should be suitably propped or supported;
- a way of restraining wheels, such as a tyre cage, should be used when inflating tyres on split-rim wheels;
- tyres should be removed from wheels before welding, cutting or heating work begins on a wheel or wheel rim fitted with a tyre, even if the tyre is deflated. See our guide *Hot work on vehicle wheels*[22] for further guidance;
- beware of the risk of explosion when draining and repairing fuel tanks, and from battery gases. Fuel tanks should never be drained or filled when the equipment is hot or in a confined space, nor should they be drained over a pit;
- take care to avoid short-circuiting batteries. Batteries should be charged in well-ventilated areas. Suitable personal protective equipment should be provided and used for handling battery acid;
- measures should be taken to prevent maintenance staff from breathing asbestos dust from brake and clutch lining pads;
- only people who have received the relevant information, instruction and training should be allowed to carry out maintenance work.

610 Fitting further features to existing vehicles ('retrofitting') needs careful planning:

- retrofitting must not significantly weaken the chassis or body structure;
- in particular, you should not consider drilling holes in the chassis and welding to it without the approval of the original manufacturer;
- retrofitting should also take account of the structure of the vehicle. Sensitive points such as fuel tanks will need to be avoided.

Lift trucks and 'thorough examination'

611 Lift trucks are used very widely in many different types of workplace. There are many different types of lift truck.

612 By law, lifting equipment must be 'thoroughly examined' at appropriate intervals to make sure it is safe to use. This includes the lifting gear on lift trucks.

613 The intervals between thorough examinations should be either:

- in line with an examination scheme drawn up by a 'competent person' (see paragraph 614), who must be independent from line managers. The competent person can be in-house or from an outside organisation such as an insurance company; or
- at least every 12 months, unless the truck operates for more than 40 hours a week, is used to lift people, or has a side shift or attachments fitted. By law, these must be thoroughly examined at least every six months.

614 'Competent person' in paragraph 613 means a person chosen by the employer to carry out thorough examinations based on his or her level of knowledge of the equipment, problems and their causes, methods of testing and diagnosing faults.

615 A national scheme of accredited, quality-assured examiners is run by Consolidated Fork Truck Services, and endorsed by the HSE.

616 See chapter *Preventing vehicles from overturning* for more information about roll-over prevention and protection, and operator restraints on lift trucks.

617 Guidance can also be found in *Safety in working with lift trucks*.[24]

Privately owned vehicles

618 Managers, foremen and site operators do not usually have much control over the condition of private vehicles (such as employees' cars) brought into the workplace.

619 However, private vehicles can be regulated by:

- restricting the type of vehicle allowed onto the site;
- restricting their routes;
- providing clearly signposted parking areas wherever possible, away from main routes and dangerous areas;
- enforcing speed limits; and
- making sure visiting drivers report to the site office.

620 You should make it clear to everyone that driving in the workplace calls for the same standard of care as on public roads, and often needs even more skill and care.

Safe drivers

Safe people in general

621 In a study of deaths and injuries involving site dumpers, less than half of the employers had bothered to check the drivers' competence.

622 By law, you must take account of your employees' capabilities regarding health and safety when you give them tasks.

623 The law also requires that employers must make sure employees are given adequate training to ensure health and safety:

■ when they are recruited; and
■ when they are exposed to new or increased risks in the workplace.

624 Only authorised drivers should be allowed to drive workplace vehicles.

Figure 40 Lift-truck operator looking backwards while reversing

625 Employers' procedures for recruitment, checking references, induction, training, supervision, auditing and assessing competence should make sure that workers are fit to operate the machines and attachments they use at work, in all of the environments in which they are used.

626 We recommend that the same (or higher) standards that are needed to drive on public roads should apply to choosing people employed to drive in the workplace:

■ with a few exceptions, people in the UK must be aged 17 or over and have passed a driving test;
■ drivers of large or heavy goods vehicles must, with certain exceptions, be aged 21 or over and have passed the appropriate test.

627 It is important to stress to drivers the risks of unsafe working such as driving too fast, turning too sharply or driving on unsuitable ground or slopes.

628 Drivers will often need many more skills than simply controlling a vehicle when it is moving. Many vehicles used in the workplace have very specialised attachments to do their jobs, and there are many other skills relating to loading, unloading, trimming, sheeting and so on.

629 Every driver, particularly younger or less experienced drivers, should be instructed to drive and to carry out other work responsibly and carefully.

630 You should never take for granted a person's ability to do a task safely.

Choosing drivers

631 You should choose drivers carefully.

632 Drivers should be fully able to operate the vehicle and related equipment safely, and should receive comprehensive instruction and training so that they can work safely.

633 Drivers will need to have a mature attitude and be reliable.

634 Safely operating most types of vehicle needs a reasonable level of both physical and mental fitness, and intelligence.

635 The drivers you choose should be fit enough so that being in control of the vehicle does not pose a risk to their own health and safety, or that of others. Fitness for drivers

should always be judged individually. Some less physically able people develop skills to compensate.

636 You can find detailed advice on the medical standards of fitness to drive on UK roads in the Driver and Vehicle Licensing Agency (DVLA) publication *At A Glance*.[23] These standards provide a good guide for medical fitness to control vehicles in the workplace as well.

637 You should try to match the requirements of a particular vehicle, task and situation with the fitness and abilities of the driver.

638 An example of a suitable level of fitness might be that people who use industrial lift trucks should usually be able to fully move their whole body, to allow them to maintain good awareness of hazards all around their vehicle.

639 For more information about the standards of physical fitness, and other things you should consider when choosing lift truck operators, you should read our publication *Safety in working with lift trucks*.[24] This guidance is also a good basis for choosing operators for other types of vehicle.

640 Employers, managers and supervisors should never allow anyone who is unfit through drink or drugs (prescription or otherwise) to drive any vehicle.

641 If the workplace has contractors working on site, the site operator or principal employer should take measures to make sure that they are competent to carry out their duties responsibly and carefully. An example might be asking for evidence of their capabilities from the drivers or their employers.

Driver training and competence

642 The amount of training each driver needs will depend on their previous experience and the type of work they will be doing.

643 Your risk assessment should help decide the level and amount of training needed for each type of work.

644 Drivers and other employees will probably need the most training when you have first recruited them.

645 It is essential to check what experience people have of the vehicles they will be using and the work they will be doing. Where appropriate, you should check that the information they give is true. For example, employers will usually need to check that references to training schemes and other qualifications are supported by certificates.

646 The information, instruction and training provided by the employer should cover areas of people's work activities if they may be unfamiliar to them.

Case study 11

An employee driving an all-terrain vehicle (ATV) received spinal injuries after the vehicle overturned while he reversed it down a slope.

To prevent the ATV from landing on him, the driver arched his back and pushed the ATV away from him. He was not wearing a helmet, and tried to protect himself as the vehicle overturned. He and other employees had received no training and the wearing of helmets was not enforced.

The company was issued an enforcement notice to train employees in the correct use of ATVs.

---

647 It is likely that training will need to cover the following:

■ general information about the job, for example:
  - the layout of the workplace routes;
  - how and where to report faults or hazards; and
  - procedures for reporting accidents;
■ training and checks to make sure that people can work safely. For a driver, this is likely to include:
  - making sure they know how to use the vehicle and equipment safely;
  - information about, for example, particular dangers, speed limits, parking and loading areas, procedures; and
  - making sure they know what personal protective equipment they should wear for the task they are going to do, and how they should use it. Examples might include high-visibility clothing, head protection, a driver restraint, safety boots and equipment to prevent falls;
  - information on the structure and level of supervision that will apply, and the penalties if they fail to follow instructions and safe working practices.

648 You may need to test trainees on site, even when they provide evidence of previous training or related work experience. Always check that trainees understand what they have been asked to do.

649 People lose skills if they do not use them regularly. An ongoing programme of training and refresher training will usually be necessary for all drivers and other employees, to make sure their skills continue to be up to date.

650 Even if drivers often operate vehicles, we recommend regular refresher training to make sure that drivers:

■ maintain good driving habits;
■ learn new skills where appropriate; and
■ reassess their abilities.

651 You should consider a gap between training and refresher training of between three to five years, depending on the risks. Some companies provide refresher training more often than this.

652 Changes in the workplace may mean that drivers or other employees are exposed to different risks. Everyone should receive suitable safety training before being exposed to risks.

653 Training is particularly important for maintenance and repair work, as these are a major source of injuries and deaths.

654 It is important to keep training records for each employee. These should include enough information to be able to identify the employee, the full training history, planned training, and a copy or details of any certificates or qualifications gained.

655 As an employer, if you are satisfied that an employee is competent to use a type of vehicle safely, you can store these details and refer to them when necessary to make sure that employees are trained and competent before being allowed to operate particular vehicles. This could be a simple document with details of the types of vehicles (or the specific vehicles) that a person is competent to operate.

656 You should keep the information on a central register.

657 An example of an employee training record is in Appendix 2. You could use this as the basis for your own records, or just photocopy it and use it as it is.

658 On some sites, drivers must carry a copy of their authorisation when driving a workplace vehicle (some sites issue authorisations in the form of a badge with their photograph). People should not be authorised unless the employer is satisfied that the person is competent.

659 Lift trucks in particular are a potentially dangerous type of vehicle. Every year, thousands of injuries involving lift trucks are reported. Accidents involving lift trucks are often associated with a lack of training and poor supervision.

660 The Health and Safety Commission has published an Approved Code of Practice (ACOP) and guidance called *Rider-operated lift trucks. Operator training.*[25] This sets the legal minimum standard of basic training people should receive before they are allowed to operate certain types of lift truck – even if they only operate the equipment occasionally. It also provides detailed guidance about how this standard can be met.

661 The ACOP covers stacking rider-operated lift trucks, including articulated steering truck types. 'Rider-operated' means any truck that can carry an operator and includes trucks controlled from both seated and stand-on positions.

662 If you employ anyone to operate a lift truck covered by the ACOP, you should make sure that operators have been trained to the standard set out there. For more information on the types of lift truck covered, refer to the ACOP.

663 The Health and Safety Commission recognises specific industry organisations as competent to accredit and monitor training providers who train instructors and train, test and issue certificates for operators.

664 These organisations accredit and monitor training providers against the standards set out in the ACOP. You can find a list of these recognised accrediting bodies in the ACOP.

665 Training courses provided by companies accredited by one of the recognised accrediting bodies are recognised by the Health and Safety Commission as meeting the legal minimum standard set out in the ACOP. Certificates from accredited training providers will normally identify the relevant accrediting body.

Operational guidance

Reversing

Common risks

666 Nearly a quarter of all deaths involving vehicles at work happen during reversing. Many other reversing accidents cause injury or expensive damage.

667 Visibility is the main problem. In many vehicles, especially larger industrial ones, it is very difficult for the driver to see backwards.

668 There are a number of steps you can take to help reduce the risk of reversing accidents. The following are examples, but it is unlikely that any single measure will be enough to protect people's safety.

Figure 41 'Danger – Reversing vehicles' sign

Safe site

669 The most effective way of dealing with the risks caused by reversing is to remove the need for reversing.

670 One-way systems are a very effective way of dealing with the risk of reversing accidents. Ring roads, drive-through loading and unloading positions, and parking areas with entrances and exits on either side are just a few examples of measures which help to prevent the need for reversing.

671 If reversing cannot be avoided, routes should be organised to reduce as far as possible the need for reversing and the distance vehicles have to travel backwards.

672 Site layouts can be designed (or amended) to increase visibility for drivers and pedestrians, and to allow plenty of room for reversing manoeuvres. The space allowed may need to be increased to improve safety. You may also need to provide reversing areas.

673 Reversing areas should be planned out and clearly marked, and should be very clear to drivers and other people. Areas can be marked out on the ground, and with clear signs to stop pedestrians.

674 The site layout should make sure that pedestrians keep well clear of reversing vehicles.

Figure 42 An example of a 'Pedestrians prohibited' sign

675 Reversing should only take place where there is enough light for drivers and pedestrians to clearly see what is happening.

676 Fitting fixed mirrors or other visibility aids in the workplace can improve visibility around vehicles.

677 Effective signs alerting drivers to the dangers of reversing, and any necessary precautions, can improve the attention drivers pay to safety (especially visiting drivers).

678 See chapter *A safe site* for more information on organising traffic systems and manoeuvring areas for safety.

679 Where vehicles reverse up to structures or edges (for example, loading, delivery or parking areas), barriers, buffers, bollards and wheel stops can be used to warn drivers that they need to stop. Even if a collision does happen, these measures can help prevent more serious injury or structural damage. They should be highly visible, and sensibly positioned. Flexible barriers may be an option and can prevent damage to vehicles.

680 White lines or guide rails on the floor can help the driver position the vehicle accurately.

Safe vehicles

681 Vehicles may have 'blind spots' – areas around the vehicle that the driver may not be able to see, because they are blocked by parts of the vehicle. However, there are many solutions to improve the driver's field of vision. See *Visibility from vehicles and reversing aids* (paragraphs 550-570) for more information.

Safe drivers

682 People should stay well clear of reversing areas.

683 You should only consider employing a banksman or signaller where there is no other way to control reversing risks. To do their job they have to stand close to where a vehicle is reversing, which can put them at risk.

684 By law, signallers in Great Britain must use certain hand signals, and employers must make sure that the correct signals are used.

685 The signals in Figure 44 are standard signals used across Europe, and should be used for guiding most vehicles around a workplace. All drivers and banksmen should know them.

686 Hand signals should be faster to show that an operation should happen quickly.

687 Hand signals should be slower to show that an operation should happen slowly.

688 These signals may not be enough to cover every situation. The law also allows for specific alternatives to be used if they are more appropriate, including BS 6736:1986 *Code of practice for hand signalling for use in agricultural operations.*[26] If these signals are not enough, further signals can be used based on existing signalling practice.

689 Whatever signals are going to be used, banksmen and drivers should clearly agree before guided manoeuvring begins.

Figure 43 Reversing guides separating loading bays and pedestrian areas

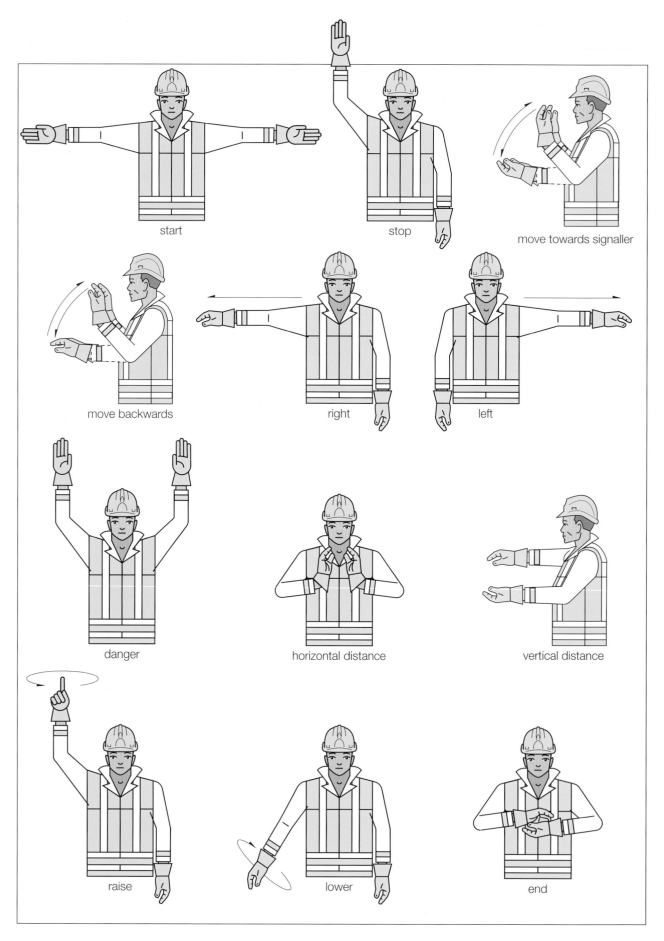

Figure 44 European standard signals for directing vehicles

690 It is important that hand signals are used consistently throughout the workplace. All employees involved in guiding vehicles should be trained as appropriate, especially new employees, who may have used a different system before.

691 Banksmen need to be visible to drivers at all times. Precautions for visibility are especially relevant in low-light conditions, which should be avoided if possible.

692 The precautions should include (where appropriate) the following:

- high-visibility equipment (vests, arm or cuff bands, gloves, bats, batons or flags). Banksmen are sometimes given a high-visibility vest of a different colour to other site workers, to help distinguish them;
- vehicle- or site-fixed visibility aids (such as mirrors).

693 Banksmen will need to stand in a safe position from which to guide the reversing vehicle without being in its way.

694 If drivers lose sight of a banksman, they should know to stop immediately. In some circumstances, portable radios or similar communication systems can be helpful, although the banksman will still need to be visible to the driver at all times.

695 Some employers (for example, quarries) do not allow banksmen to be used due to the size of vehicles involved and the difficulty that drivers have in seeing them.

696 If drivers are not able to see clearly behind the vehicle for any reason, they should apply the brakes and stop the engine, leave the cab and check behind the vehicle before reversing. In a busy place this precaution may not be enough, because people can move behind a vehicle after the driver has returned to the cab. Segregating pedestrians and vehicles, and improving the ability of the driver to see around the vehicle from the driving position, are more effective ways of improving pedestrian safety during reversing.

697 Where banksmen are to be used, they must be available when they are needed.

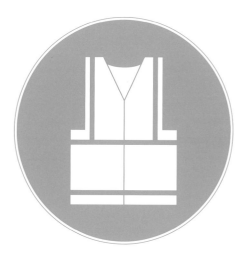

Figure 45 Example of mandatory 'high visibility vest must be worn' sign

698 Everyone involved in reversing should be trained and competent. You should identify all the people who are involved, and take account of their abilities when allocating tasks and deciding what training they should receive. Specific training may be needed to deal with reversing or using reversing aids fitted to vehicles.

Parking

Common risks

699 Carelessly parked vehicles can injure and kill people. A vehicle parked on a slope can move if all of the brakes are not used properly. It can take very little slope to make a vehicle move, and it can sometimes happen even if the vehicle has been still for some time.

700 People can be hit by moving vehicles, run over or crushed against other objects. These risks are likely to be much worse when the vehicle is out of control. Drivers are often hurt trying to get back into moving vehicles to properly apply brakes. If people are working on a vehicle that begins to move, they could fall.

701 Even if no one is hurt, a vehicle can hit other vehicles, buildings, scaffolding and so on, causing serious and expensive damage.

702 Carelessly parked vehicles can reduce visibility for drivers and pedestrians, and can force pedestrians onto vehicle routes if they block a path.

Safe site

703 Wherever possible, there should be designated parking areas in the workplace. Parking areas should be:

- level;
- firm;
- well lit;
- clearly marked and with safe walking areas;
- easy to find; and
- as close as possible to where people need to go when they leave their vehicles.

Case study 12

A bus driver was run over and killed by a double-decker bus while he walking across the depot yard.

It was dark and raining, and the driver had just parked his bus. The company had not controlled the risks that resulted from vehicle movement in the yard. They failed to segregate vehicles and pedestrians, had not provided suitable signs and road markings, and the lighting was poor.

The bus company were prosecuted and fined £50 000 with £15 000 costs.

---

704 See *Parking areas* (paragraphs 409-427) for advice about physical precautions to reduce parking risks.

Safe vehicles

705 Vehicles should be parked on firm and level ground, preferably in a parking area (see paragraphs 699-704). A piece of ground may look flat, but it only needs a slight gradient for a vehicle to move if the parking brakes are not applied.

706 A vehicle should not be left unless the parking brakes have been firmly applied, the engine has stopped, the starter key has been removed, and any mounted equipment has been lowered to the ground or secured. Remember the following:

- brakes ON;
- engine OFF;
- key OUT;
- equipment SAFE.

707 Where vehicles have to be parked on a slope:

- all brakes should be applied;
- the vehicle should be left in gear (if it is safe to do so);
- wheel chocks or stops should be used where appropriate; and
- vehicles should usually be parked facing up or down the slope, not sideways on. There are some exceptions to this, for example, where operators are working directly in front of the vehicle pointing downhill (such as a farm worker opening a gate), it may be safer to park across the slope in case the brakes fail to prevent the vehicle from moving.

708 It is important to lock away the keys of vehicles left parked in workplaces overnight, at weekends or when they are being left for long periods.

Safe drivers

709 Drivers should always be competent. They should understand the risks of leaving a vehicle parked badly, and how to avoid doing this. In particular, drivers should be instructed and monitored in the way they use vehicle and trailer brakes.

710 People in control of workplaces where trailers are parked need to make sure that drivers are aware that both tractive unit and semi-trailer parking brakes should be used when parking. Drivers' behaviour should be supervised and monitored.

711 Trailer parking brakes are there because they need to be, and must be used every time a vehicle and trailer are parked. You should consider signs, instruction and any other measures to make sure this happens.

712 See chapter *Coupling and uncoupling* for more information on trailer brakes.

Coupling and uncoupling

Common risks

713 Coupling and uncoupling trailers is a common activity, and one with serious risks if it is not carried out safely.

714 Most accidents during coupling involve drivers or other people being run over, hit or crushed by moving vehicles or trailers – often while trying to get back into a cab to apply the brakes.

715 There may be a significant risk of falling during coupling or uncoupling, especially in the dark.

716 If proper care is not taken to use a suitable place to couple or uncouple, poor ground may cause a vehicle or trailer to overturn, or the trailer can move, especially on a slope. A piece of ground may look flat, but it needs only a slight slope for a vehicle or trailer to move if the parking brakes are not applied. Trailers can begin to move even if they have been still for some time.

717 During uncoupling, the trailer will move from being supported by the tractive unit to bearing its own full weight. This can cause the trailer to sink into soft ground or topple over. The combination must be parked on ground that is firm enough to support the weight of the trailer (including pressure from the landing legs).

718 Drivers often leave the engine running and the parking brake off when coupling or uncoupling hoses. This is very unsafe. As best practice, drivers should not leave the cab without turning off the engine, applying the brakes and, where possible, removing the keys.

719 'Fail-safe' emergency air-pressure brakes lock vehicle wheels when an air hose is disconnected from the trailer (for example, if in a crash the trailer breaks away from the cab, the line would be broken and the emergency brakes would be applied, stopping the trailer). Drivers sometimes use the emergency brake as a parking brake, by disconnecting the airline ('dropping the red line') rather than by applying the trailer parking brake. This is very dangerous and should never happen.

720 Emergency brakes can't be relied on as parking brakes. Air pressure drops over time as braking systems leak air, reducing the ability of the emergency brakes to hold the semi-trailer. Also, reconnecting the hose can free the brakes immediately, leaving the semi-trailer free to move with the driver away from the cab (especially if, for any reason, the tractive unit parking brake has not been applied).

Safe site

721 Hauliers and site operators should make sure that areas where coupling and uncoupling take place are well lit, firm and level.

722 Lighting is especially important where coupling or uncoupling happens away from sunlight (including at night). There is a significant risk of the driver falling when carrying out coupling or uncoupling operations in darkness, as they may be less able to see slippery surfaces, hazards or where steps are.

723 Also, drivers are likely to need plenty of light to check that locking pins and safety clips are in place, and any cables and hoses have been properly attached.

Safe vehicles

724 Hauliers and site operators should make sure that wheel-stops, handholds and vehicle lighting (for example, at the back of the cab) are provided wherever appropriate.

Figure 46 Footholds are provided on this tractive unit to make it easier and safer to access the rear of the cab

725 If coupling may happen away from outside lighting, vehicle owners should consider fitting outside lighting to the vehicle itself (especially behind the cab) to provide a safer working environment.

726 There should be safe access to the 'fifth wheel' area (the area behind the cab, where the trailer connects to the tractive unit). This should include steps up to the area, and a catwalk that provides good grip (bear in mind that there may be oil leaks). The area behind the cab should be kept clean and clear to make slipping or tripping less likely. Drivers should know how to move any hinged fairings to make access to this area easier, and should do so.

727 It is sometimes not possible to connect hoses after coupling (for example, 'close-coupled' combinations such as 'reefer' trailers, where the temperature control unit fixed to the front of the trailer means no one can get access to the fifth wheel area). A risk assessment should recognise the risks involved in connecting the hoses before coupling ('split coupling'), and a safe system of work should be in place to reduce risks.

Safe drivers

728 Employers should make sure that everyone involved in coupling or uncoupling is aware of safety procedures, and should check that they understand how to use the equipment safely.

729 Employers should provide suitable gloves, footwear, and other personal protective equipment such as high visibility clothing, where appropriate, to protect people working on or around vehicles, including people involved in coupling. Workers should use this equipment as part of a safe system of work. There is more information about avoiding falls in *Preventing falls from workplace vehicles*.

730 Make sure the following coupling procedures have been followed wherever possible:

(a) the trailer handbrake should be applied (if fitted). The absence of handbrakes is **only** acceptable if the trailer air brakes are fail-safe or there are other measures to prevent movement;

(b) for automatic coupling:
- the cab should be reversed slowly under the trailer, with the 'kingpin' lined up to the 'V' of the locking mechanism. Listen to hear the fifth wheel lock onto the kingpin;

(c) for manual coupling:
- reverse the vehicle into place;
- make sure that the parking brakes are applied;
- manually attach the locking mechanism;

(d) do a 'tug test'. Try to drive forward slowly in a low gear to check that the fifth wheel is in place;

(e) make sure that the parking brakes are applied;

(f) leave the cab and inspect the locking mechanism to make sure that it is secure;

(g) fit any safety clips and connect all brake hoses and the electrical supply to the trailer. Check that they are secure;

(h) wind up any landing legs on the trailer and secure the handle;

(i) fit the number plates and check that the lights work;

(j) release the trailer handbrake (if there is one).

Uncoupling

731 When uncoupling, you should normally follow the procedure in paragraph 730 in reverse order, using brakes and stabilisers as appropriate. Always remember to set the tractive unit parking brake before leaving the cab.

732 Before uncoupling, also check that:

■ the ground is firm and level enough to support both the landing legs;
■ the parking brake is set on the trailer.

733 After uncoupling, check that the landing legs are fully extended, locked in place, are properly padded and are not sinking into the surface.

734 See our free guidance *Parking large goods vehicles safely*[27] for more information on coupling safely.

Loading and unloading, and load safety

Common risks

735 Loading and unloading can be very dangerous. Machinery can seriously hurt people. Heavy loads, moving or overturning vehicles and working at height can all lead to fatal or serious injuries.

736 One of the four most common types of vehicle accident at work is people being hit by objects falling from vehicles.

737 People involved in loading or unloading often work close to moving lift trucks, which pose a high risk of hitting them or otherwise injuring them.

738 You should pay particular attention to the dangers of high loads that might have to pass under bridges, overhead power cables, parts of buildings, pipework, trees, and so on. These can catch loads or high vehicles, causing serious accidents (often involving falling loads).

739 The heavier the load, the greater the chance of it shifting when being transported. The weight of a load alone can't be relied on to stop it shifting. For example, dust, dirt or oil on the loading surface can reduce the amount of grip a load has, and can make it much more likely to slide around when being transported.

740 It is much harder to stop a load once it has started to shift. Keeping the load still on the vehicle (and, where possible, secure) is the best way to make sure it does not shift dangerously.

741 It is common practice to use sheeting hooks to secure loads. These hooks are not designed to bear heavy loads, and may be in the wrong places to secure a load safely. They should never be used for this purpose.

742 Communication is very important for safe loading and unloading. There may be several people involved, often working for different employers and sometimes even speaking different languages.

743 Loading in a way that will allow for efficient unloading (for example, in reverse delivery order) will cut down the amount of double handling.

Case study 13

The driver of a lift truck was injured when he was struck by a pallet falling from the back of the goods vehicle he was unloading.

The goods vehicle was loaded with pallets of flat-packed cardboard boxes, packed three pallets high. The forks did not reach high enough to unload the top pallet, so the driver tried to unload the top two pallets in one go. The top pallet toppled and fell approximately 3 m, hitting the driver.

The lift truck did not have enough reach and was therefore not suitable for the task. A lift truck with protection against falling objects was also needed for work where objects could fall on the driver. It is the employer's responsibility to provide equipment that is suitable for its intended use.

744 You should provide a safe place where drivers can wait if they are not involved. See paragraphs 463-466 for more guidance about welfare provisions for visiting drivers.

745 Information in this guide about sheeting and unsheeting will also be relevant, both for making sure that loads are safely secured and that employees are working safely.

746 Avoid the need for people to walk on top of vehicles or loads wherever possible. No one should stand on a load once it is attached to lifting equipment (such as cranes or a fork-lift truck).

Safe site

747 Vehicles reversing before loading or unloading are a major risk. If possible, remove the need for reversing with 'drive-through' loading areas as part of an overall one-way system.

748 Loading and unloading areas should be:

- clear of passing traffic, pedestrians and other people who are not involved in loading or unloading;
- clear of overhead pipework or electricity cables so that there is no chance of fouling them, or of electricity jumping to 'earth' through machinery, loads or people; and
- level – to maintain stability, vehicles and their trailers should be on firm ground, free from potholes or debris, which could make vehicles unstable.

749 See chapter *A safe site* for more information on organising a safe place for loading and unloading.

750 Safety equipment may be needed. For example, guards or skirting plates may be needed if there is a risk of anything being caught in machinery (such as dock levellers or vehicle tail lifts).

751 Appropriate signs and road markings showing safety equipment, showing the areas pedestrians are not allowed in, and alerting people to loading and unloading operations should be in place and visible, wherever appropriate.

752 There should be safeguards against drivers accidentally driving away too early. This does happen and can be extremely dangerous. See chapters *A safe site* and *Safe vehicles* for advice about preventing ways to make sure this doesn't happen.

Safe vehicles

753 The vehicle should be able to take the full weight of everything it is asked to carry. This will include any loading or unloading machinery, such as a fork-lift truck used to help unloading.

754 No vehicle should ever be loaded beyond its 'rated capacity' (the manufacturer should provide this information) or its legal limit of gross weight if it is to be used on public roads. Overloaded vehicles can become unstable and difficult to steer, or be less able to brake.

755 Some parts of a vehicle can take more weight than others. Think about how the different parts of a vehicle are arranged underneath the loading surface. Where is there the most support for a load or for a piece of loading machinery?

756 Before loading, check the load platform, bodywork and anchor points to make sure that they are suitable for the load, are clean and are in a good working order. Debris, broken boarding, rusted anchor points, dust (particularly brick dust) or oil that may cause a slip could all pose a risk to safety.

757 Some loads (such as bricks or rubble) leave a dust behind that can make loads slip while they are being transported. To improve load safety, drivers may need to thoroughly sweep the vehicle bed before loading.

758 Wherever possible, loads should be carried separately from passengers. If the cab is not separate from the load area (for example, a closed van), a bulkhead should be fitted between the load compartment and the cab, which should be strong enough to withstand a load shifting forwards in an emergency.

759 The most suitable securing method should be used for different types of load.

760 Operators should make sure they have the correct securing equipment for the types of load carried. Where general cargoes are carried, various types should be available.

761 Clamps, special bolts, steel-wire ropes, chains, webbing harnesses, sheets, nets, ropes and shoring bars are all suitable to secure loads, but it is essential to make sure that they are strong enough for the weight of the loads carried.

762 Sheeting rope hooks should never be used to secure loads. They are not designed to bear heavy loads and may be in the wrong position to secure a load safely.

763 Sheets themselves are only suitable for restraining loads if they have been designed for this. See chapter *Trimming, sheeting and netting* for more information.

764 You should use sleeves and corner protectors to prevent damage to both the load and the lashing or sheet if it passes over a sharp corner.

765 Lashings (such as ropes, webbing, chains, cables, clamps) should be in good condition and be able to withstand all normal forces. Lashings should be properly tightened at all times, although not overtightened as this can damage the lashings.

766 Some goods are difficult to restrain while they are being transported. Loads should be suitably packaged. Where pallets are used, the driver will need to check that:

- they are in good condition;
- loads are properly secured to them; and
- loads are safe on the vehicle. They may need to be securely attached to make sure that they cannot fall off.

767 It is best for the individual parts of a load to be packed closely together. If this is not possible, some type of packing (commonly known as 'dunnage') should be used to fill any gaps.

768 A number of materials are suitable for use as dunnage. The most common are timber, folded cardboard, hardboard, high-density foam and air bags. Dunnage should take up as much of the empty space as possible.

769 You should take care not to damage the load by using unsuitable dunnage. As a result, the type of load being carried will influence the dunnage material you choose.

770 For more detailed and specific guidance about securing different types of load (such as steel, timber, loose bricks), and load safety in general, see the free Department for Transport Code of Practice *Safety of Loads on Vehicles*.[18]

771 Tailgates and sideboards should be closed wherever possible.

772 All items of loose equipment (such as sheets, ropes, dunnage, rope ends) should be securely restrained at all times, whether or not they are being used.

773 If you cannot avoid a load overhanging the edge of the vehicle, the overhang should be kept to as little as possible and should be suitably marked.

774 The driver should make checks before unloading to make sure that loads have not shifted while they are being transported and are not likely to move or fall when restraints are removed.

775 Every driver should know what to do to deal with any load that has moved dangerously, including what equipment is needed. They should be able to advise workers dealing with a dangerously shifted load (including the emergency services). A solution may be as simple as pushing the load off the vehicle from the opposite side, with appropriate equipment and precautions.

776 Wherever possible, a safe area away from other work should be available for vehicles carrying unsafe loads to be quarantined. A competent person should decide upon a safe system of work before anyone tries to deal with an unsafe load. Vehicles carrying unsafe loads should not be sent back onto public roads if they are unsafe to travel.

777 As a general rule, goods carried in curtain-sided vehicles should be secured as if they were being carried on an open, flatbed vehicle:

■ A curtain is a thin, flexible sheet, and even when it is reinforced it can usually only resist a moving load by bulging outwards. If this happens when the vehicle is moving, it could make the vehicle unstable and cause an accident.
■ If the curtains have been designed to secure loads, the weight of the maximum load should be clearly marked. If no mark can be seen, it should be assumed that the curtains cannot bear loads and, as far as securing loads is concerned, may as well not be there.
■ Before the curtains are closed, the load and its lashings should be thoroughly checked for safety. This final check is important, as it can be very difficult to check during the journey with the curtain sides in place.
■ If the curtain bulges, showing that the load has shifted, the curtain should not be opened. Access should be gained to the load compartment through another route – possibly through the back door or through a curtain on the other side of the vehicle. The safety, stability and security of the load should then be assessed before unloading takes place.
■ There are several different ways the strain a load is placing on a curtain could be safely worked out. You could consider opening half a curtain, getting into the vehicle from a different place or even undoing only every other strap.

778 Not all bulging curtains show that a load has shifted. It is possible that a load has been well secured, and the sheet stretched over it. The driver will need to be aware of how the curtains should look, so that they can judge safety during the journey and when they arrive.

779 Curtain-sided trucks are often unloaded during darkness – for example, during the early morning in winter. Drivers should be ready to feel along curtains and tap at bulges. Ideally, unloading should always happen in places with enough lighting for this to be unnecessary. Outside lighting or hand-held torches or lamps can help identify the condition of a load.

Figure 47 Securing rollcages in a curtainsider

780 Loads should be secured or arranged so that they do not slide around. Racking may make loads more stable.

781 Curtain-sided vehicles are often unloaded using fork-lift trucks, as they are very suitable vehicles for moving loads on pallets.

782 Wherever fork-lift trucks are used, you should make sure drivers are aware of the trucks, are kept out of harm's way and do not drive away while the fork-lift truck is still unloading.

783 When using fork-lift trucks, it is essential to consider:

- how much the truck can lift;
- the size and spread of the forks; and
- the ground the truck is being used on.

784 It is essential that the vehicle and any attachment used for a job are suitable.

785 Long items can fall off forks if they are not balanced properly and, in particular, if the forks are too close together. Also, they may fall off the forks if the truck is driven too quickly around corners or over rough ground.

786 Attachments such as side-shift forks and load clamps can help to make sure that long loads can be handled safely. As well as being trained in using the trucks and their attachments, drivers should also be competent to handle routinely supplied long or awkwardly shaped items and should be instructed in safe systems of work.

Safe drivers

787 Drivers should be given clear instructions and training on how to safely secure every type of load they carry.

788 Both site workers and delivery drivers should be prepared to refuse to allow loading or unloading (or to stop loading or unloading) if they think risks demand this. They should know that they will have the support of their employer if they do this. Everyone involved in a delivery or collection should agree to this principle when arrangements are being made.

789 The delivery driver should not use any equipment (including lift trucks) at a delivery or collection site unless this has been agreed beforehand and steps have been taken to make sure that the equipment is well maintained and the site is suitable. Lift trucks and other specialist vehicles should only be used by trained drivers. If the driver does use a lift truck, they must be trained to the standards described in *Driver training and competence* (paragraphs 642-665). Employers should be confident that drivers are able to work safely.

790 Loading and unloading will often involve mechanical lifting. By law, you must make sure that all lifting operations are properly planned by a competent person, appropriately supervised and carried out safely. (See definition of competent person in paragraph 614.)

791 Lifting equipment needs to be suitable for its use, marked with its safe working load, properly maintained, inspected appropriately and thoroughly examined regularly.

Figure 48 Fork-lift truck loading a curtainsider

792 Planning is the key to safe loading, safe unloading and load safety.

793 See the sections on delivery safety in the chapter *Organising for safety* (paragraphs 182-227) for advice about planning a delivery.

easy, safe access to toilet and refreshment facilities reduces risks considerably. A safe area may be needed for drivers to watch the loading or unloading.

799 Workers who do need to be in the same area as loading or unloading (for example people who are involved in

Figure 49 Vehicle unloading from firm and level ground

794 If more than one company is involved, they should agree beforehand how loading and unloading will happen. For example, if visiting drivers unload their vehicles themselves, they should receive the necessary instructions, equipment and co-operation for safe unloading. Arrangements will need to be agreed beforehand between the haulier and the person receiving the delivery.

795 If employees of more than one company are involved in loading or unloading a vehicle, that vehicle should be considered a shared workplace while the loading or unloading is taking place.

796 See the sections on deliveries in the chapter *Organising for safety* (paragraphs 182-227) for further information on co-operating between suppliers, hauliers and people receiving deliveries. See paragraphs 172-181 for more information about shared workplaces.

797 No one should be around during loading or unloading if they are not needed.

798 It is often unrealistic and sometimes unsafe to expect drivers to stay in their cab while their vehicle is being loaded or unloaded. A designated safe area for visiting drivers with

the work) should be segregated from vehicle movement wherever this can reasonably be achieved, and specific systems of work should be applied to make sure the driver does not move the vehicle unless everyone involved is known to be in a safe place.

800 The vehicle should be as level, stable and stationary as possible. All of the vehicle and trailer brakes should be applied and any stabilisers should always be used.

801 Wherever possible during loading, follow these principles:

■ loads should be spread as evenly as possible during loading, moving and unloading. Unbalanced loads can make the vehicle or trailer unstable, or overload individual axles. See paragraphs 839-841 for advice about trimming a load to make sure it is evenly balanced;

■ balancing the load is important to make sure the trailer moves predictably and safely;

■ generally, loads should rest as close as possible to the bulkhead;

■ however, avoid loading drawbar trailers too far forwards, because this can lead to a snaking effect as the combination moves forwards;

- avoid loading to the back of the trailer, because this can cause the trailer to tip backwards (especially for single-axle trailers). This can reduce the grip the vehicle has on the road surface, as the wheels are lifted away from the ground;
- loads should be arranged close to the middle of the trailer and slightly forward of it to place enough downward force on the tow bar to keep the trailer coupled, but not enough to put too much pressure on the tow vehicle suspension or hitch;
- loads should be balanced across the axle (or axles) of a drawbar trailer so that coupling or uncoupling can be managed easily and safely, and so that the trailer is stable when being transported;
- wherever possible, drawbar trailers should be coupled (or uncoupled) unloaded, as this makes them easier to handle and generally safer to work with.

reduce the risk of a fall. If the load has to be sheeted or unsheeted, an on-vehicle sheeting device that can be worked from ground level or a safe place higher up should be provided, or a sheeting platform or gantry should be available on site.

807 In some workplaces, it may be practical to fit a harness system to protect people working at height, such as an 'inertia-reel fall-arrest' system (where harnesses are worn linked to overhead rails).

808 See chapters *Trimming, sheeting and netting* and *Preventing falls from workplace vehicles* for more information.

809 If you provide fall-arrest systems, you should consider signs showing that they must be used and should monitor their use.

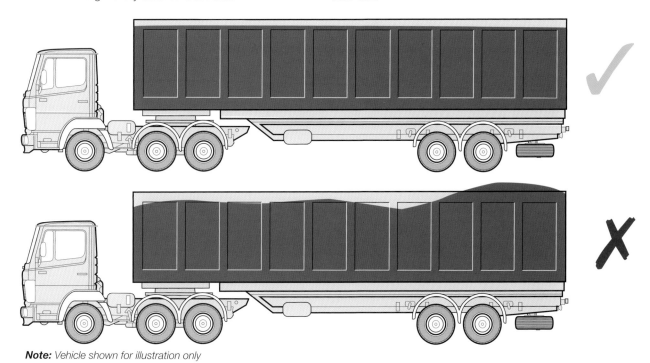

Note: *Vehicle shown for illustration only*

Figure 50 Loads should be spread evenly across the vehicle

802 Unbalanced single-axle trailers are also dangerous as they can tilt dangerously during coupling or uncoupling, shifting loads or trapping anything underneath.

803 Loads gathered right at the front and back of a trailer may be safely balanced, but can be harder to control when being transported as the weight distribution causes the trailer to swing out further than a trailer loaded towards the centre of gravity.

804 Normally, the load should be arranged so that it does not block the driver's field of vision, including the rear view through the mirrors.

805 No one should ever stand on a load to balance it on the forks of a fork-lift truck.

806 If workers are going to need to climb onto the vehicle or be supported by the load (or both), you may need to

810 Equipment or parts of the vehicle can also fall or be dislodged during loading or unloading. Workers should know how to prevent this from happening.

Figure 51 'Safety harnesses must be worn' and 'Industrial vehicles operating' signs

Trimming, sheeting and netting

Common risks

811 Some loads will need trimming to make sure they are well balanced and ready to be transported, or before they can be sheeted or netted. Trimming is often needed where bucket or hopper loading has left a load unevenly spread in the vehicle container.

812 Trimming a load can involve climbing to a height that makes accessing the load possible, but as usual should not need anyone to actually walk on a load if this can be avoided.

813 There are a number of reasons you may want or need to cover a load, and sheeting or netting is often a good way of doing this.

814 Some materials may need to be kept hot while being transported, such as bitumen or asphalt. Other loads need to be kept dry, such as quicklime or some other powders.

815 There are also legal duties to cover some types of load to:

■   protect the environment;
■   prevent them from being a nuisance when you go onto public roads (for example, material being blown off); or
■   keep them safe.

816 Loads need to be properly secured, and sheets or nets might be part of the way you do this.

817 Sheeting, netting or removing sheets or nets can be dangerous, especially when it is carried out by hand.

818 Rain or ice can make vehicle surfaces or the top of a load slippery, risking a fall.

819 Trimming or covering a load can involve being in a high place. Chapter *Preventing falls from workplace vehicles* provides more information on the dangers involved in working in high places.

820 Loads can be uneven or unstable, so no one should walk on them if possible. Loads might appear solid, but there might be gaps (known as 'voids') under the surface of aggregate loads, or gaps between stacked bags or pallets. Loads might also present other dangers, such as dangerous contents, high temperatures, sharp edges or dust and fumes.

821 If sheeting or unsheeting happens somewhere windy, gusts can catch sheets or knock workers off balance.

822 Sheets can be heavy or difficult to manage, causing strains or sprains, or doing damage to workers over time. Sheets can get very heavy if they are wet or if a load sticks to them.

823 Drivers sometimes walk backwards in dangerous places during sheeting or netting, such as close to the back or sides of a vehicle.

824 Working at height can involve being near dangerous objects, such as hot vertical exhausts or overhead power lines.

825 Torn sheets or nets, breaking ropes or straps, or other accidents can all put workers off balance and cause falls.

826 Sheets or nets can flap around if they are not properly secured. If large loads are being covered, they may need more than one sheet. The places where two sheets join can be opened up by the wind, which can disturb the load and let wind and rain under the sheet.

827 Loads can move when being transported. This can be especially dangerous when a driver arrives and begins to unsheet the load.

828 Sheeting often involves working in the same area as fork-lift trucks, which may be involved in other activities but still pose a risk to people involved in sheeting or unsheeting.

829 If a driver of a tipper lorry discharges the load with the sheet still on, air might not be able to replace the load. If this happens, a vacuum can form behind the load, which can break the sheeting system.

830 You should take effective measures to make sure sheeting and netting is as safe as possible, within reason. You need to take account of the types of load and vehicle, how often sheeting or unsheeting happens and other specific characteristics of the workplace.

831 During loading, unloading and sheeting, vehicles that are used by employees of more than one company should be considered 'shared workplaces', and so suitable arrangements for safety should be made by everyone concerned. This will involve the different companies co-operating with each other. See *Deliveries – communication* (paragraphs 203-227) for more information on safety in shared workplaces.

832 Wherever you can, remove the need for covering loads. Ask yourself if the load actually needs sheeting or netting. If it is safe to leave a load without a covering, and if road and environmental law allows it, you can avoid sheeting or netting altogether.

833 You may also need to speak to customers and suppliers about the need for covering loads. Some companies expect loads to be sheeted even if this is not really needed. You should be avoiding manually sheeting or netting wherever possible, and you may need to explain to someone receiving a delivery why the load will not be covered with a sheet or a net.

834 Try to find other ways of protecting a load, such as protecting each unit separately (for example, shrink wrapping) or choosing loads prepacked in protective sacks or containers.

835 You can also avoid sheeting by using other vehicles such as curtain-siders, and containers that do not need sheeting. Enclosed 'demountables' (for example, skips with tight lids), shipping containers and intermediate bulk carriers (IBCs) are all alternatives to open-load bodies.

836 If sheeting is only done to secure a load, you should find another way that doesn't involve someone climbing on the vehicle or load. See chapter *Loading and unloading, and load safety* for more information on securing loads.

837 You should not sheet vehicles by hand unless it is not 'reasonably practicable' to use automated sheeting systems or sheet from the ground. Wherever possible, the need for people to climb onto vehicles should be avoided. You should not require workers to climb a vehicle to sheet by hand unless it is not 'reasonably practicable' to use automated sheeting systems or sheet from the ground.

838 The following points should be considered, whatever method of sheeting is used:

- Do not overload the vehicle and try to load evenly to avoid the need for trimming. You could use the loading shovel to load evenly along the length of the vehicle (not in peaks), or use it to pat down the load to flatten peaks.
- Train and instruct staff on safe systems of work (and provide refresher training where necessary) for using the automated sheeting, manual sheeting, platforms and personal protective equipment. Sheeting and unsheeting should be supervised and monitored.
- You should provide gloves and safety boots, and make sure that people use eye and head protection.
- Regularly check that sheets are in good condition, and are replaced when necessary. Visually check straps and ropes used for pulling and securing the sheet.
- Sheeting mechanisms, platforms, gantries and fall-arrest equipment (like harnesses and lanyards) should all be regularly inspected, repaired and maintained.

Safe site

839 You should provide suitable tools for trimming loads. A rake is often used and will need to be long and strong.

840 Platforms are very suitable for trimming loads. They would normally be fixed in drive-past or drive-through arrangements, where vehicles can be parked alongside a stable structure and the load can be accessed safely.

841 Platforms can also be used to improve safety during sheeting or netting, although these activities may need more access to the vehicle than trimming.

842 Loads can be sheeted from platforms, removing the need to climb onto the vehicle or the load. For more information about access platforms, see *Site-based access to vehicles* (paragraphs 498-522).

843 However it is done, sheeting and unsheeting should be carried out in designated places, away from passing traffic and pedestrians and, where possible, sheltered from strong winds and bad weather. Extra care will need to be taken in wet or icy conditions.

844 Sheeting and unsheeting should happen as close to loading or unloading areas as possible, to help protect loads and reduce the chances of loads being caught by the wind.

845 Ropes, straps and sheets can snap or rip. The driver should avoid leaning backwards when pulling the sheet tight and should never do so close to the sides or end of the vehicle.

846 Vehicles should be parked on level ground, with their parking brakes on and the ignition key removed.

847 Vehicles should be sheeted before leaving the site.

Safe vehicles

848 If you can't avoid the need to cover loads, you should use mechanical sheeting methods that avoid people walking on vehicles or loads wherever this is reasonable.

849 Think about mechanical sheeting systems when you negotiate new contracts with hauliers or when you consider new vehicles. They can also often be fitted onto existing vehicles.

850 Mechanical sheeting systems normally allow sheeting and unsheeting from ground level or from the cab.

851 Apart from reducing risks, mechanical sheeting systems can avoid the need for expensive gantries or platforms, and will be available at the destination as they are usually fixed to the vehicle.

852 Sheeting systems can also save money by greatly reducing the turnaround time of vehicles on site, and by creating more streamlined loads (saving time and fuel).

853 Mechanical sheeting systems can be fully automatic or operated by hand. Fully-automatic systems are better because the driver can usually be somewhere safe and doesn't have to strain.

854 Many mechanical systems spread a traditional sheet across the load, either from end to end or from side to side, or by spreading it from the centre to the sides. There are several common types:

- many systems involve a sheet on a roller, mounted on a mast behind the cab. The sheet is then dragged out over the load, by mechanised arms on the trailer, or sometimes just by a rope being pulled. Special care needs to be taken when these systems are used in windy conditions;

■ tightened wires on pulleys, running along the top of the vehicle sides. A sheet is attached to them like a washing line, and moving the wires can either cover or uncover the load. This system is cheap and effective, but can be stopped by heaped loads, and the gathered sheet can take up a lot of space. Other problems include the sheet not making a complete seal over the load, and the sheet flapping when it is not being used (this strains the equipment).

855 There are several different types of fully automatic systems for covering a loads that don't use traditional sheets:

■ 'spray sheeting' involves covering a load with a liquid that hardens into a protective shell. This would usually take place at the weighbridge, where the operator can decide the extent of spraying. Spray sheeting will replace the need for sheeting or unsheeting, but involves a cost for every spraying and cannot be used on all loads (for example, quicklime cannot be spray covered);

■ panel systems can extend from the back of the cab, unfolding over the top of a container or the body of the vehicle. These can completely remove the risks to drivers involved in sheeting or unsheeting. There are other problems you should consider, such as overloaded or protruding loads preventing the panels from closing completely or the panels dislodging items that could fall.

856 There are many systems that partly automate sheeting, making the job safer for the driver. They are often like the automatic systems for normal sheets mentioned above, but with some effort needed from the driver to move the sheet:

■ some systems use runners over the front and back ends of the trailer, allowing the operator to pull the sheet across the load from the side;

■ crank handles are another popular solution, allowing drivers to move the sheet from the ground.

857 Most of these systems need the operator to secure the sheet at the sides if a proper seal is needed.

858 No matter what type of sheeting equipment is fitted or used, there should always be safe access onto and down from the vehicle if people have to climb. Using well-designed and well-positioned fixed ladders and handholds can improve access.

859 For more information about safe access to vehicles, see *Site-based access to vehicles* (paragraphs 498-522) and chapter *Preventing falls from workplace vehicles*.

860 Sheets should be:

■ large enough to cover the load with a large overlap (at least 6 inches) of the tailgate and sides;

■ in good condition to avoid tearing, which can throw a person off balance (you should check the sheets regularly); and

■ as light as possible for the purpose, to make handling them safer.

861 Some lightweight sheets allow air to pass through, making them less likely to catch in the wind. There may be a loss of waterproofing, but this should be considered if it is practical.

862 Tarpaulins only protect against the weather and so should not be used to secure a load if they are used as load sheets.

863 Purpose-made load sheets (which include webbing straps) have a 'rated load capacity' and can be used to secure a load up to that weight.

864 If in doubt, you should assume that a sheet is not strong enough to secure a load.

865 See chapter *Loading, safe unloading and load safety* for further information on securing loads.

866 If you use nets:

■ they should never be used to secure a load beyond their maximum rated capacity;

■ they should be properly tightened, as instructed by the manufacturer; and

■ the mesh size should be less than the smallest item the net is expected to hold (although this will not always apply to nets used over loose bulk loads).

867 Ropes and straps should be:

■ in good condition and inspected regularly;

■ long enough to be tied to the anchor points that are designed for this (straps should not be left hanging loose); and

■ heavy and strong enough not to be pulled loose by the wind under the sheeting.

Safe drivers

868 If you cannot avoid manual sheeting or netting, is it possible to do it from the ground? Open skips should always be covered at ground level, before they are lifted.

869 Using a net instead of a sheet can also help with flatbed vehicles, because the net will be lighter and can often be thrown over the load from the ground.

870 If you cannot avoid manual sheeting or do it from ground level, you should use platforms or gantries with harness systems to help make sheeting safer. As these measures stay on sites, they may not be available when the sheet or net is removed at the destination.

871 A platform can help sheeting workers avoid walking on a vehicle or load, but won't normally protect against falls from the platform itself.

872 You can find more information on platforms and gantries in *Site-based access to vehicles* (paragraphs 498-522).

873 Workers must be competent in the use of protective equipment such as harness systems. They should have received appropriate practical and theory training from a competent person before they need to use the equipment.

874 You should also provide training and information to workers using sheeting systems, sheets and nets.

875 You should provide (and make sure that people use) gloves, safety boots and eye and head protection.

876 Regularly supervising sheeting, unsheeting and netting is vital to make sure safe ways of working are being followed.

877 If more than one sheet is needed to cover a load, the rear sheet needs to be put in place first, to make sure that overlaps don't face forwards allowing wind and rain to get between the sheets. Try to make sure that the wind will close any gaps or folds in the sheet rather than open them up. The same principle should be applied to folds at the front or on the sides of the vehicle.

878 If you cannot avoid sheeting by hand:

- avoid the need for a person to go on top of the load wherever possible (for example, with platforms or gantries);
- where platforms are provided, you should make sure there are enough of them, and their use should be supervised and monitored;
- mudguards and wheels should not be used as steps; and
- you should provide suitable safety arrangements (as set out in this guide).

879 If manual sheeting on the vehicle is the only option, you must provide a suitable fall-arrest system for everyone to use. These do not prevent someone from falling but should reduce the risk of serious injury if someone does.

880 If there are no fall precautions in place at the site, the driver should refuse to sheet the vehicle manually by climbing, and should turn back. Drivers should be aware that managers will support this decision. This also applies to delivering loads where there are no precautions available for unsheeting.

881 Drivers should check what facilities will be available before they allow loading to begin, to make sure unnecessary loading and unloading does not take place.

882 It is sensible for hauliers to check the facilities at both ends of a journey when arrangements are first being made.

883 When pulling sheeting, nets or ropes, the driver should always have one foot behind the other to avoid overbalancing.

884 For more information about laying your site and traffic routes out for safe vehicle use, see chapter *A safe site*.

885 If harnesses and lanyards are to be used, drivers must be trained in what checks to carry out before using them and how to use the personal protective equipment.

886 Use the following procedure for manual sheeting with a harness system (the sheet should already be suitably folded in a position to the front of the vehicle on a sheet rack or purpose-built shelf or on carrier hooks):

- The driver should walk forwards down the centre of the load towards the back of the vehicle, rolling out the folded top sheet.
- When halfway along the load (but at least 2 m from the back of the vehicle), the driver should turn around and pull the sheet tight. It is important that the sheet is not pulled at any other time.
- The driver should turn again and, facing the rear of the vehicle, throw the rest of the sheet and ties over the tailgate.
- Standing at the centre of the load, the driver should then open out the sheet, throwing the sheet and ties over the sides of the vehicle.
- The driver should then return to the front of the vehicle by walking forwards along the centre of the load, and return to the ground using any access features on the vehicle.

887 Although systems of work can be put in place to prevent people from needing to leave ground level during normal sheeting, people carrying out inspection or maintenance work on sheeting systems may have to leave ground level. Safety precautions need to be in place to protect these people.

Tipping

Common risks

888 Tipping can be dangerous, especially if it is not done carefully.

889 Each year, a significant number of tipping vehicles (including rigid-body lorries, tipping trailers and tankers) overturn. Overturns usually have the potential to kill people. Overturns can be the result of a number of different problems:

- Poorly maintained tipping vehicles and under-trained operators are common causes of accidents during tipping.
- Imbalanced loads can make vehicles unstable. There are a lot of reasons why a load can be imbalanced, including bad loading or trimming, shifting, or parts of the load 'freezing' during tipping (becoming stuck in the upper part of the tipping body, above the centre of gravity).
- Loads can shift around and settle while being transported – especially bulk powder, flakes, grains, rubble etc. This can make different parts of the vehicle heavier, and can also lead to different parts of the load freezing during tipping, which can put the vehicle off balance. There may be a higher risk of this if a load has different densities, such as builders' rubble.
- Uneven tipping surfaces can put a vehicle off balance, or unsuitable ground can give way, especially under very heavy vehicles.
- Tipping often involves reversing, sometimes towards steep slopes. Vehicles can reverse too far. There are also the usual risks caused by poor visibility during reversing, such as hitting people or other objects.
- Tipping lorries can hit overhead obstructions. These can include power lines, with the risk of electrifying the vehicle and any people who touch it.

890 Loads can be very dangerous as they are unloaded.

891 If the vehicle has not been properly prepared, discharging loads can damage parts such as hatches or tailgates, or a quickly sliding load can cause a vacuum behind it, which can suck in sheeting and damage the vehicle.

892 If a load is too high for a bar across the discharge area, it can stick or break the bar.

893 If the load does strike the tailgate with more force than the vehicle is designed to manage, it could break the tailgate, or force the tipping body to break away from the tipping ram and be thrown backwards.

894 Some tipper lorries have partitioned bodies, to keep sections of load separate. Partitioned loads need to be handled with caution, and care needs to be taken to keep loads well distributed and to make sure that axles are not overloaded.

895 Partitions should never be released while the body is tipped, as different parts of the vehicle may not be able to deal with the effect of the moving load and the vehicle balance can be seriously affected.

896 There is a risk that partition doors (especially at the back of the vehicle) can spring open if too much weight is put against them.

897 People should be kept well clear, to avoid being hit by loads.

898 A load being released though a sleeve, pipe, chute or nozzle can create static electricity, which can present very significant risks of starting a fire or an explosion where there are combustible loads, or can shock people.

899 Some tipping operations use specific equipment to help the delivery, such as earthing straps, grills and guards on intake pits, overfill alarms on silos, and 'pneumatic conveyance' systems. There may be specific risks that result from using this equipment, especially if it is not used correctly.

900 Delivery drivers sometimes rest part of the delivery equipment on the ground to provide an improvised earthing route for electricity, instead of using any proper earthing arrangements (for example, an earthing strap). This is very dangerous and should never happen.

901 There is a risk of slipping or tripping on loads spilled during tipping.

902 A load that might form a cloud (such as flour or other fine powders) if tipping happens without a good seal can present a wider risk of explosion, and can also cause breathing problems for workers.

903 Refined oil could also explode because of a spark, and other types of load are dangerous in themselves.

Safe site

904 Tipping operations should be carried out on ground that is level and stable, and clear of overhead hazards such as power lines, pipework and so on. A general rule is to make sure there is at least 9 m clearance overhead, although ideally there will be nothing at all overhead.

905 Tipping areas should be well lit so that drivers and other people involved can clearly see any problems.

906 It will not usually be possible to completely avoid reversing where tipping has to happen. However, you should think about reducing the amount of reversing to as little as possible. See chapter *Reversing* for more information.

907 At sites where level and stable tipping places can't always be guaranteed (such as waste disposal sites), you will need to make sure that tipping faces are suitable and safe (for example, by making sure that the faces are well compacted, and that there are no significant side slopes).

908 The vehicle should stay level if it is moved forward during tipping.

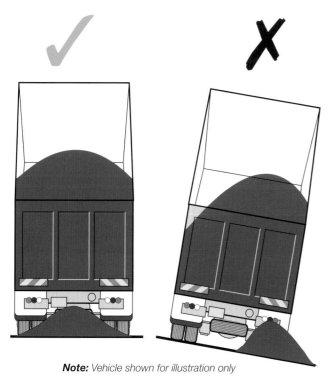

Note: Vehicle shown for illustration only

Figure 52 Vehicles should be parked on level ground

909 Articulated vehicles should always be tipped with the tractive unit and trailer in line. There will always need to be enough space for a vehicle to manoeuvre the trailer and cab so that they are lined up.

910 Wherever possible, and particularly where reversing needs to happen, wheel stops that are large enough to let the driver know to stop should be used, to help position vehicles correctly.

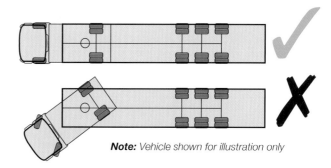

Note: Vehicle shown for illustration only

Figure 53 Articulated vehicles should be parked straight

911 For tipping over unsupported embankments or faces, the wheel stop will need to be far enough from the edge to make sure the weight of the vehicle does not make the ground collapse.

912 If the load is released through a chute, pipe or nozzle, there is a risk that static electricity can build up. It may be necessary to consider an earthing strap between the delivery chute (or pipe or nozzle) and the receiving vessel to earth this charge. This should always be used, and drivers should never rely on improvised earthing arrangements.

913 Risks are especially high where potentially explosive loads (such as powders or refined oil products) are being delivered, as an electric spark could ignite these. Effective earthing can reduce these risks.

914 If the load is being released into a silo or a bin, some type of alarm (usually a sound alarm) may be needed to tell staff that the container is full. Sound alarms should be loud enough to be heard from wherever the operator stays during tipping.

915 If the load is being released into a hatch or a pit that someone could fall into, there should be a mesh or a guard over the hole to prevent this from happening.

Safe vehicles

916 You should consider using vehicles that avoid the need for tipping. Vehicles with load bodies that 'eject' a load without needing to tip may be suitable – for example, 'walking floor' load bodies.

917 Every vehicle should have information about safe operating limits (such as load capacity, height and width, ground clearance, tipping load) in the cab.

918 Loads put significant stress on the door and door lock of containers, which can result in the door springing open or the load being ejected.

919 Some older designs mean that the driver has to stand behind the door while opening it. This is a dangerous position if the door flies open or if the load spills out. You should make sure that drivers can operate the door locks in safety from the side of containers and that doors will not spring open when released.

920 If a load takes up more than one compartment of a vehicle with partitioning doors, it should still be partitioned. To make sure that doors are only being used to control the weight they have been designed for, **all** doors must be used and locked.

921 If partition doors are not used, the rear doors can spring open under the pressure of the load.

922 Rear doors of the 'barn door' type should be secured in the open position before tipping.

923 The tailgate should be released before tipping and removed if necessary.

924 For grain or other similar deliveries, where a 'grain hatch' allows the driver to release a certain amount of the load before releasing the tailgate, the hatch should be opened and the flow allowed to stop completely before continuing to open the tailgate.

925 Where tailgates are not removed and the load is released through an opening or a hatch, the tailgate latch or securing mechanism should be strong enough to withstand the full effect of a released load (otherwise it may get damaged when a load hits it, and not be safe for further use).

926 If you are using a 'pneumatic conveyance' system:

- trained operators should always be available to operate equipment;
- open vents to bins and silos should be open to the atmosphere;
- fill alarms should always be in place and used; and
- if a cloud of powder gathers, it can be explosive or cause breathing difficulties. This should always be avoided.

927 The 'power take off' (often known as the PTO), which shifts power from the road wheels to the tipping pump, should never be used if the vehicle is in gear.

928 When the engine power is routed to the tipping pump, the driver should take care not to over speed the pump (by over-revving the engine), which can cause the pump to seize if it runs out of oil.

929 We do not recommend using 'donkey engines' to drive the tipping mechanism, as the driver has to stay outside the cab and in a potentially dangerous area while the load discharges.

930 Various restraining devices are used to secure doors open, including rigid hook and eye, chain fastening, or 'non-captive' locking devices. Single rear doors weigh about 500 kg and tipping with the bin inclined at 50° to 60° puts a significant load on these restraining devices.

931 Maintain the locks, door handles, restraining devices and hinges, and make sure they are adequate for the purpose. Never use baling wire or string to secure bin doors.

932 Where possible, consider single-door containers with side-release locking mechanisms to reduce the number of moving parts.

Safe drivers

933 You can remove the risks to people who do not need to be in the tipping area by making sure that they are kept completely clear.

934 Drivers should be trained in safe tipping, and should understand the limits of what their vehicle can do safely.

935 Drivers should be given full details of the load and delivery conditions, including how they can get there safely (avoiding low or weak bridges), and who they should report to.

936 Drivers should be able to refuse to begin tipping (or any other operation) if they are not satisfied that it is safe to do so. They should be confident that they would have the full backing of their employer if they need to refuse to do anything for safety reasons.

937 Employers should also allow whoever is in charge of tipping to stop it for safety reasons, and they should be confident that their employer would support their authority. This authority can be included in contracts.

938 When tipping is being arranged, both the haulier and the person receiving the load should exchange written information about the load, safe tipping, the characteristics of the site, a safe route to the site, and safe ways of working. The driver and workers at the receiving site should be made aware of this information as well, and before the delivery begins. See *Deliveries - communication* (paragraphs 203-227) for more guidance about exchanging information.

939 Drivers visiting a site should have to report to the site operator for any relevant instructions.

940 Weather can be a significant factor in tipping. If the surface is very slippery, there may be a risk of a person or vehicle losing their grip, and windy places can also cause problems. Everyone should be prepared to wait for wind to die down to safe levels if it poses a risk to safe tipping.

941 The receiving site operator should appoint someone to be responsible for tipping. That person should be fully informed about tipping safety (and other safety matters relating to vehicle movements and visiting drivers), and should be prepared to stop any operation if they are not satisfied about safety. That person will need to be confident that their employer would support a decision to stop tipping for safety reasons.

942 If the load is to be released into bins or silos, the driver will need to make sure they are filling the correct containers and that there is enough room for the load before they begin to tip.

943 The site operator and the visiting driver need to co-operate to keep unnecessary people or vehicles away from the tipping area.

944 You should consider normal reversing safety – see chapter *Reversing* for more information.

945 Drivers should never begin tipping until they have received a specific instruction to do so, or have followed other agreed safety procedures to make sure it is safe to release the load.

946 Before tipping starts, the driver may need to check that the load is evenly distributed across the vehicle. This is particularly important where:

- the load might have slipped sideways or too far forwards, risking overloading the tipping gear;
- the load shifting sideways or backwards could make the vehicle topple over; or
- there is a risk of the load 'freezing' down one side as a result of movement or settling. If this happens, that side could cause an imbalance and cause the vehicle to topple. Care needs to be taken that the load is released evenly.

947 Sheets should be loosened enough to make sure that a vacuum will not form behind the discharging load.

948 The driver may also need to check that the load will release smoothly and safely and that it cannot jam under the tailgate if the load is higher than the top of the tailgate.

949 When raising or lowering the body, the driver should never leave the vehicle and should make sure that the cab doors are closed.

950 The driver should never stand or walk immediately behind the vehicle (or allow anyone to do so) when the body is raised during tipping. There is also a risk that a load being released unevenly could cause the vehicle to tip sideways, and drivers should be aware that this can happen.

951 Vehicles should never approach overhead cables if this can be avoided, and should never touch them. It is not always possible to tell what type of cable has been fouled in this way – some older power cables look like telephone wires. See our leaflet *Working safely near overhead power lines*[28] for further guidance about safety in this area.

952 If an overhead cable is touched, and the situation cannot be made safe immediately:

- the driver should leave the vehicle by jumping as far clear as possible;
- the driver should **never** make contact with the ground and the vehicle (or anything touching the vehicle) at the same time as this could complete an electrical circuit and may cause serious injury or death;
- the driver should immediately make sure that no one else comes into contact with the vehicle or anything touching it, while it is still touching the cable; and
- the surrounding area should be secured immediately and the local electricity supplier contacted to arrange for the power supply to be cut off. If you do not know the electricity supplier's number, call 999.

953 The driver should be able to tell when the body is fully tipped, and should stop the tipping pump as soon as possible and release the tipping gear.

954 The driver should never go beneath a tipped trailer that is only supported by lifting gear. If a driver cannot avoid reaching underneath a raised body, it should be securely propped first.

955 Drivers should receive training and instruction in how to anticipate loads sticking or 'freezing' in the body.

956 Some loads are particularly likely to freeze. Mechanical aids (such as 'vibratory discharge' systems) may be needed in some cases.

957 If a load does freeze, the body needs to be lowered and the rest of the load loosened before the body is raised again.

958 The operator should never try to dislodge a frozen load without lowering the body first.

Case study 14

A self-employed lorry driver suffered a broken leg when scrap steel fell from the trailer of his vehicle.

Some scrap steel had stuck in the vehicle trailer after tipping. The driver re-tipped the trailer and then, without lowering the trailer, walked round behind it to check that the scrap was discharged. Some scrap dislodged and fell on to him.

When he realised that some scrap had stuck in the trailer, the driver should have lowered the trailer body and freed the remaining load before re-tipping.

---

959 The driver should always give the vehicle a wide berth around the sides and at the back, in case a stuck load suddenly moves.

960 The vehicle should never be driven to shake free a stuck load. No one should enter the body of a tipper lorry to free a stuck load while the body is raised, as there is a risk of the load falling and harming someone.

961 Drivers should also not have to hold onto a pipe or a nozzle, as this places them in a dangerous position, close to both the discharging load and to any static build-up.

962 Drivers should pay attention to filling gauges and alarms wherever appropriate.

963 Drivers should not be expected to work in areas where there is a lot of dust, without an appropriate mask.

964 Spilled loads of any kind should be avoided and should be cleaned up as soon as it is safe to do so.

965 After releasing the load the driver should always make sure that the body is completely empty.

966 The driver should not drive more than a few metres forward to make sure the load is clear, and should only do this after checking that the load is at the bottom of the tipped body. If the driver has to leave the cab to do this, they should fully apply the brakes, turn off the engine and (if possible) remove the keys. Again, the vehicle will always need to be given a wide berth.

967 The engine power should never be shifted back to the road wheels while the tipping pump is still in gear.

968 If the vehicle begins to topple over, the driver should brace themselves against the back of the driver's seat and hold firmly on to the steering wheel. The driver should never try to jump out of a lorry that is falling over.

969 You should give drivers a safe place and plenty of time to make sure that their vehicle is safe to use after tipping. This could include sweeping any remaining load out of the back, which might need a suitable place away from pedestrian routes.

Preventing vehicles from overturning

Common risks

970 Vehicle overturns cause nearly a fifth of all deaths related to workplace transport.

971 Fork-lift trucks, tractors, compact dumpers, tipper lorries, forestry and all-terrain vehicles and cranes are all especially likely to overturn.

972 People responsible for a workplace need to examine which vehicles are being used, where and how.

Case study 15

A worker died when his vehicle toppled over an unprotected edge.

A weighbridge was set near the entrance of a waste-handling site. It was raised about 30 cm above the level of the surrounding ground, and had no edge protection.

An employee driving a 2.5 tonne counterbalance lift truck followed regular practice and drove across the elevated weighbridge when a trailer blocked the normal site access road. The rear left wheel went over a 22 cm vertical edge and the truck toppled onto its side. The truck was not fitted with a seat belt, and the driver died when his head was struck by part of the lift truck frame.

Risk assessments had identified the potential for overturning – and the lack of a seatbelt – but no remedial action had been taken. The firm was prosecuted and fined.

973 There are a lot of reasons vehicles might overturn. They include:

- travelling on slopes that are too steep;
- going over slippery surfaces (such as oil or grease patches);
- going over soft ground, potholes or uneven terrain;
- going over kerbs, steps or other edges;
- being overloaded or, for lift trucks such as fork-lift trucks, under-loaded (they may be designed to be more stable when loaded);
- being unevenly loaded;
- going too quickly, especially around corners;

- not being suitable for the task; and
- carrying loads at a dangerous height (for example, with a lift truck load fully raised).

974 You should think about ways of making overturns less likely, and ways to make the consequences of an overturn less serious.

Safe site

975 You should plan out suitable routes, avoiding too steep slopes, uneven or slippery surfaces, kerbs, sharp turns and anything else that would make the vehicle unstable.

976 Barriers, walls, banks and signs can all help drivers avoid unsuitable terrain or hazards such as pits or trenches.

977 Road humps can be used to control speed, but there should be a warning sign or mark before them. Lift trucks should avoid having to pass over road humps (unless they are of a type that can go over them safely). This may mean planning lift truck routes that do not pass over speed bumps.

978 You should consider speed restrictions and enforce them where appropriate.

Safe vehicles

979 By law, many types of vehicle must have a 'roll-over protection system' (ROPS) and restraints fitted if there is a risk of them overturning. ROPS can mean roll cages, roll bars or other types of protective structure. An ROPS will not prevent an overturn, but it should make a serious injury less likely – especially when operator restraints are also used.

980 If there is a risk of anyone being hurt if a vehicle rolls over, you must do one of these things:

- make sure the vehicle is stable;
- make sure that, if possible, the vehicle remains upright, or can do no more than roll onto its side;
- put in place a structure to protect anyone on the vehicle if it does roll further than onto its side (ie roll all the way over) – such as an ROPS.

981 The only exceptions are:

- vehicles that are not significantly likely to overturn;
- vehicles where these measures would increase risks to safety, make the vehicle useless or would not be practicable; and

Figure 54 Site dumper with ROPS

■ counterbalanced lift trucks that can carry no more than 10 tonnes and which are controlled by a centrally-seated operator (the mast will normally prevent these machines from rolling further than their sides).

982 If there is a risk of a vehicle crushing anyone it is carrying if it rolls over (whether or not an ROPS is fitted), the employer must make sure that there is a restraining system to prevent anyone on the vehicle from being thrown under it.

983 If your risk assessment finds that any vehicle in your workplace is at risk of overturning, the following free information sheets can give you more detailed guidance about what you need to do:

■ *Hiring and leasing out of plant: Application of PUWER 98, regulations 26 and 27;*[29]
■ *Retrofitting of roll-over protective structures, restraining systems and their attachment points to mobile work equipment;*[30]
■ *Fitting and use of restraining systems on lift trucks.*[31]

984 All-terrain vehicles (ATVs) often work in a different way to other vehicles. Overturn risks can be different for ATVs. See our free publication *Safe use of all-terrain vehicles (ATVs) in agriculture and* forestry[32] for further information.

985 Our publication *Safe use of work equipment*[33] also provides more detailed information about what the law says on reducing the risks to safety caused by overturning vehicles.

986 There are other vehicle issues that can be important in preventing overturns:

■ brakes need to be connected and working properly;
■ if brakes are independent of one another (for example, on some tractors), they need to be properly balanced;
■ tyres should always be inflated to the correct pressure, have good tread and generally be in good condition;
■ lubricant and hydraulic fluid levels, and pneumatic pressure levels, should be regularly monitored.

987 Under no circumstances should any vehicle be loaded beyond its capacity. Overloaded vehicles can become unstable and difficult to steer, or be less able to brake.

988 Loads should be evenly distributed across the vehicle and be adequately secured. Shifting loads can make a vehicle very unstable. See chapter *Trimming, sheeting and netting* for information on safety during load trimming.

989 Loads should only be carried by vehicles that are suited to the specific task.

990 See chapter *Loading and unloading, and load safety* for further information on suitable vehicles and general load safety.

991 An unloaded lift truck will normally be less stable than when it is loaded. Operators should be properly trained, informed and supervised to handle the vehicle safely.

992 Loads should be carried in a lowered position wherever possible.

993 For spreading vehicles (for example, tractors towing spraying equipment), remember that a load that gets lighter will mean less grip against driving surfaces. Liquid loads are especially dangerous on sloping ground if they surge around in their container.

Safe drivers

994 Vehicles should only be driven over surfaces they are designed to cope with.

995 Vehicles should not be used in a way that risks an overturn, whether or not an ROPS and seat restraints are fitted.

996 Vehicles should be driven at a suitable speed for the task, load, terrain and type of vehicle.

997 Where driving across a slope cannot be avoided, drivers should always try to drive forwards up the slope, and should pay special attention to loose ground, humps and so on. If the vehicle is off-balance already, a much smaller object can overturn it.

998 If driving down a slope cannot be avoided, drivers should try to drive carefully down the shallowest part of the slope. It may be better to drive forward down the slope rather than diagonally, to keep the sideways stability of the vehicle.

999 In particular, do not turn down a slope while you are on it.

1000 Remember that vehicles are often more stable going uphill than downhill. Being safe to drive up a slope does not mean it will be safe to drive down it.

1001 Keep away from banks, ditches, pits and kerbs, especially when turning.

1002   Site operators and employers should check that workers are wearing seat restraints, and are not taking risks that might cause vehicles to overturn. Where seat restraints are fitted, they should usually be worn at all times. An exception might be warehouse lift truck operators picking orders in a warehouse (or similar work), where the surface is good, the vehicles move slowly, and workers need to get in and out of the vehicle frequently. A risk assessment should identify whether risks are low enough for seat restraints not to be worn.

1003   Only drivers trained to recognise and avoid a risk of overturning should be allowed to use vehicles.

1004   Site operators and employers should make sure that proper information is available on where and how seat restraints and other safety equipment should be used. This could include signs on safety areas and vehicles, clear floor markings and adequate training.

1005   In many situations, the driver restraint is simply to prevent the driver from trying to jump off an overturning vehicle and being crushed by the ROPS or FOPS (falling object protection system). If a vehicle begins to topple over, the driver should brace themselves against the back of the driver's seat and hold firmly onto a secure part inside the cab. The driver should never try to jump out of a vehicle that is falling over.

1006   An ROPS on some kinds of vehicle can reduce the risk of injury if it overturns, but is not fully effective unless the driver is also wearing an appropriate restraint (for example, a seat belt). Drivers have been killed when a vehicle with a roll cage overturned, because they were not wearing the restraint provided.

1007   Drivers should be trained to follow safety procedures, wear proper restraints for their safety, and spot dangers and avoid them.

1008   If an employer has taken reasonable steps to monitor and enforce the wearing of restraints where they are appropriate, drivers who do not wear the restraint (or who carry passengers who do not do so) could be prosecuted.

Preventing falls from workplace vehicles

Common risks

1009   Falls from vehicles are among the most common accidents involving workplace transport.

1010   Falls can be caused by many things, such as:

- slipping and falling from loads and access steps and ladders;
- broken ropes or torn sheets causing overbalancing;
- inappropriate footwear;
- bad weather; or
- a lack of awareness and training.

1011   Even falling a short distance can be very serious, or even kill someone, so you have a legal duty to try to prevent falls.

1012   By law, employers must take suitable and effective measures to:

- prevent anyone from falling a distance that is likely to hurt them; and
- prevent anyone from being hit by a falling object that is likely to hurt them.

1013   Where people working for different employers work in the same place, those employers may have a legal duty to work together to make sure they are meeting their legal responsibilities. See paragraphs 172-181 for more information about shared workplaces.

1014   Your risk assessment should include things that might involve a person climbing onto a vehicle or a structure for a transport-related activity. You should remember to include irregular or less frequent activities involving someone getting to less easily reached parts of the vehicle (such as the engine, exhaust stacks or refrigeration units) for maintenance or other reasons. You should still consider measures to deal with significant risks resulting from this work. See chapter *Managing the risks* for more information about this.

1015   By law employers must consider a hierarchy of different ways of controlling the risks from working at height so they choose the safest option for the work.

1016   Work in high places should be avoided wherever possible. You can do this by using gauges and controls that are accessible from the ground. For example, where a road tanker delivers fuel to a petrol station, the employer of the delivery driver and the station operator should consider whether 'dipping' (which means the driver must go onto the top of the vehicle) is necessary.

1017   Automatic sheeting systems (often known as 'easysheets') are another example of an effective way of avoiding the need for workers to climb on vehicles. See paragraphs 848-858 for more information about automatic sheeting systems.

1018   You should give permission to gain access onto vehicles only to people who cannot avoid doing so.

1019   If the work at height cannot be avoided, it is best for people to be protected by equipment and site or vehicle features that prevent falls. If equipment to prevent falls is being used, the best solutions are those that protect everyone, not just individuals.

1020   If only one person is at risk, harness systems, for example, might be most appropriate.

1021   You should instruct and train workers to use the work equipment competently, and provide information for workers. You should be doing this anyway – safe ways of working should always be part of managing risks.

1022   You should assess how much light is available for people climbing into or onto vehicles, or walking on vehicles. Poor visibility can lead to accidents. Hand-held lights or torches would not normally be an effective way of lighting places where people need to use their hands.

1023   People climbing onto vehicles or other structures should always use the 'three-point hold' rule. This means they should try to keep at least three points of contact with the vehicle they are climbing (with their hands and feet), moving one limb at a time and testing the new hold before moving on. Looping an elbow around a support is not a secure enough hold – people should use their hands to grasp supports. The three-point hold rule is less important for people using stairs, although handholds are still important.

1024   Tasks that are carried out from ladders or steps should allow the worker to keep the centre of their body between the sides of the ladder or steps, and both feet on the same rung or step. Only tasks that are of a short duration and are low risk should be carried out from ladders.

1025 Employers should consider other sections of this guidance for operations that might involve a risk of falling. Information about safety during loading and unloading, sheeting operations, coupling and uncoupling, and other areas are all likely to be relevant.

Safe sites

1026 Platforms or gantries at places where vehicles often need to be accessed (for example, for loading, unloading or sheeting) can also avoid the need to climb on top of vehicles or loads. See *Site-based access to vehicles* (paragraphs 498-522) for more information about this.

1027 You should also consider the following:

■ vehicles should be parked on firm and level ground wherever possible, to make sure that other safety precautions are effective;

■ too much mud can make rungs, steps and walkways slippery and unsafe for people getting onto (or off) a vehicle;

■ other permanent features can be used to prevent people from climbing on vehicles. Examples include stairs folding out from a fixed platform, or a stepped wall to allow drivers to walk up to their cab;

■ gusts of wind can knock workers off balance, or affect opened doors or hatches on vehicles. You should recognise the effects of strong wind and deal with them if necessary.

1028 If work has to be carried out higher than ground level, and permanent, safe access cannot be achieved using platforms, gantries or other site measures, you should arrange other types of safe access.

1029 Moveable steps (not attached to the vehicle) are safer to climb than vehicle-mounted ladders. You can find more information about vehicle-based access in paragraphs 1031-1041.

1030 You should also consider signs showing trip, slip, fall or other general hazards wherever there is a significant risk of an accident. However, the signs must not be used in so many places that they become part of the 'background' and are ignored.

Safe vehicles

1031 Access should be by a well-constructed ladder or steps.

1032 Ladders or steps should be well built, properly maintained and securely fixed.

1033 You should avoid using suspended steps wherever possible. If you cannot avoid using them, you should use rubber or cable suspension ladders, not ladders made of chains.

1034 Ladders and steps should slope inwards towards the top if this is 'reasonably practicable'. They should not lean outwards towards the top.

1035 Rungs or steps on vehicles should have the same features as those on site-based ladders or stairs. This means that they should:

■ be level and comfortable to use;

■ have a slip-resistant surface; and

■ should not allow, for example, mud, grease or oil to build up dangerously (for example, grating could be used to allow things to pass through a step).

1036 For more information on safe ladders, steps and platforms, see *Site-based access to vehicles* (paragraphs 498-522).

1037 The first rung or step should be close enough to the ground to be easily reached – ideally about 40 cm, and never more than 70 cm.

1038 If fixed to a vehicle, ladders or steps should be placed on the front or back of the part of the vehicle that needs to be accessed, as close to the relevant part of the vehicle as possible.

Figure 55 This piece of plant has a good access system, with steps and handholds. The first step is flexible to stop it being damaged in rough conditions

1039 Opening (and holding open) a cab door on a vehicle should not force a driver to break the 'three-point hold' rule or to move to an unsafe position.

1040 Access doesn't always have to be through the side of the semi-trailer or the cab. The 'fifth wheel' area behind the cab of a tractive unit can be used as long there is a properly designed cover and the area is free of things that might lead to a person slipping or tripping, such as tools or ropes.

1041 Wherever possible, walkways should be used. Walkways should be made of slip-resistant grating (with enough space for mud or oil to pass through the grate and away from the walking surface) or another slip-resistant material.

Figure 56 This LGV is fitted with a set of foldaway steps to make accessing the load easier

1042   Walkways, steps, ladders, handrails and so on should be positioned away from wheels if possible, to prevent thrown mud from making them slippery. Mudguards can also help to keep them clean.

1043   Top and middle guard rails may be needed, to protect people when they are standing or crouching. You can consider collapsible rails that can be locked onto the access ladder.

1044   Vehicle owners need to consider fitting further safety features (such as those we have described in paragraphs 1031-1041) if they are not already present.

Figure 57 This dropside vehicle has been fitted with two footholds (one of which folds flat) and a handhold (not shown) to help workers access the load bed

1045   If features are retrofitted to existing vehicles, the alterations must not affect the structural integrity of the equipment and the actual fitting must be safe (for example, welding onto petrol tankers might be very unsafe).

1046   Lift trucks are sometimes used to lift people. Although some vehicles are designed with this in mind (for example, 'man up/man down'-type picking vehicles), many lift trucks are not.

1047   If a lift truck has not been designed specifically for this, it must be used to lift people only with purpose-designed working platforms, securely fixed to the vehicle and inspected by a competent person. Pallets should never be used as substitute working platforms.

Case study 16

A worker fell over 2 m from a pallet balanced on the forks of a lift truck.

Pallets of sacks were stored three high but had settled unevenly. This sometimes made retrieving of the top sack difficult.

Using pallets raised on the forks of a lift truck as a work platform is dangerous, and is a common cause of accidents in warehouses. Pallet racking and a safer way of accessing the sacks should have been provided.

Access should have been gained using a mobile elevated work platform, a purpose-built and properly secured lift-truck working platform, or a stepladder.

Safe drivers

1048   Employers should make sure that people working with vehicles are aware of dangers and safety precautions, and monitor how vehicles are used wherever practicable.

1049   No one should ever try to climb onto a moving vehicle.

1050   Passengers should only be allowed on a vehicle if it is designed to accommodate them safely, with suitable seating and restraints.

1051   People climbing on vehicles should always use the 'three-point hold' rule. See paragraph 1023 for more information.

1052   People walking on vehicles should always do so carefully, facing in the direction they are walking and keeping their feet well apart and free to move. They should pay attention to the stability and grip of the surfaces they are walking on.

1053   To keep their balance at all times, people working with vehicles should not lean backwards, especially near the back of a vehicle (for example, during sheeting).

Case study 17

An experienced LGV driver suffered head injuries when he fell approximately 4 m from the top of a stack of pallets loaded on to a flatbed trailer. He had climbed on top of the load to release a snagged rope used for securing the pallets.

A safe means of access to the top of the pallets should have been used, for example a mobile elevated work platform.

Climbing on top of loads should be avoided whenever 'reasonably practicable', and should not be attempted without appropriate precautions. The employer is responsible for instructing employees on the use of safe working practices.

1054   No one should rely on ropes, sheets or loads to support their weight, as they can rip, tear or move. People should only rest their weight on equipment if that is what it is intended for and it is known to be safe. If a sheet, rope or strap needs to be pulled tight, the operator should try to keep one foot behind the other, and keep control of their weight.

1055   An obstruction in the cab or elsewhere is a very common cause of falls, and spilt loads can also be very dangerous. Vehicles should be kept as clean and tidy as possible, and especially free from grease or oil on walking or other support surfaces, such as any platform area behind the cab.

1056   People should never use parts of the vehicle not designed as hand or footholds (such as mudguards, bumpers, tracks, hooks) to gain access to any part of a vehicle. Parts of the vehicle not designed to support weight may give way, and their surfaces are likely to be unsuitable.

1057   When getting down from the vehicle, people should use the steps or ladder provided. Workers should not jump down, as this can cause slips and falls, or can lead to injuries like sprained or broken ankles, or long-term knee complaints. The exception to this is workers jumping clear of vehicles where there is a risk of electric shock should they climb down.

1058   People involved in working with or around vehicles should always wear appropriate footwear, which is in good condition and has good tread and ankle support. Where a risk assessment shows that people need to wear a certain type of footwear, that footwear is considered personal protective equipment and so needs to be provided and maintained free of charge to the worker.

1059   In some workplaces it may be practical to fit a harness system to protect people working at height, such as a 'work-restraint' or an 'inertia-reel fall-arrest' system, where harnesses are worn linked to overhead rails.

1060   If you provide 'fall-arrest' systems, you should consider using signs to show that they must be used. You must also supervise and monitor their use. You must consider maintenance and provide training to users.

1061   If there is a possibility of a fall, the law requires you to plan for the rescue of anyone who has fallen.

Appendices

Appendix 1: Safety checklist

1 The following checklist shows which areas you should look at when you are identifying transport hazards in the workplace, and when you are assessing whether existing precautions are enough or if more precautions are needed.

2 It also gives some ideas for reducing the risk. The checklist will not necessarily be comprehensive or relevant for all work situations.

The workplace			
1 Check that the layout of routes is appropriate. **For example:**			
Are vehicles and pedestrians kept safely apart?	❏ Yes ❏ No		If 'No', see paragraphs *258-263*, **371-392**
Are there suitable pedestrian crossing points on vehicle routes?	❏ Yes ❏ No		If 'No', see paragraphs **378-385**
Are there suitable parking areas for all parking needs?	❏ Yes ❏ No		If 'No', see paragraphs **409-427**
Do the vehicle routes avoid sharp or blind bends?	❏ Yes ❏ No		If 'No', see paragraphs **294-296**
Is a one-way system used on vehicle routes within the workplace, where this can be achieved?	❏ Yes ❏ No		If 'No', see paragraphs **250-252**, *258*, *292*, *670*
2 Check that vehicle traffic routes are suitable for the type and quantity of vehicles that use them. **For example:**			
Are they wide enough?	❏ Yes ❏ No		If 'No', see paragraphs *258*, **261-273**, 282-286
Do they have firm and even surfaces?	❏ Yes ❏ No		If 'No', see paragraphs ***319-344**, 478-487*
Are they free from obstructions and other hazards?	❏ Yes ❏ No		If 'No', see paragraphs ***523-529***
Are they well maintained?	❏ Yes ❏ No		If 'No', see paragraphs *320*, **335-337**

Key (paragraph references):
Italic: Specific legal duty
Bold: Main reference

The workplace *(continued)*

3 Check that suitable safety features are provided where appropriate. For example:

Are roadways marked where necessary – for example, to show the right of way at road junctions?	❏ Yes ❏ No	If 'No', see paragraphs *311-312*, 388, **393-408**
Are roadsigns as set out in the Highway Code used where necessary?	❏ Yes ❏ No	If 'No', see paragraphs 229, 311-313, **393-402**
Where they are needed, have you put in place features such as fixed mirrors to provide greater vision at blind bends, road humps to reduce vehicle speeds, or barriers to keep vehicles and pedestrians apart?	❏ Yes ❏ No	If 'No', see paragraphs **296-297**, 676 (site-fixed mirrors), **351-370** (controlling speed), **371-392** (pedestrian safety)
Do visiting drivers and pedestrians report at the entrance for instructions before entering the site?	❏ Yes ❏ No	If 'No', see paragraphs 391, **619**, 939

The vehicles

4 Check that vehicles are safe and are suitable for the work they are being used for. For example:

Have suitable vehicles and attachments been chosen for the tasks that are actually carried out?	❏ Yes ❏ No	If 'No', see paragraphs
Do they have suitable and effective service and parking brakes?	❏ Yes ❏ No	If 'No', see paragraphs **577-591**, 608
Do they have suitable external mirrors and additional aids (eg CCTV) where necessary to provide the greatest visibility when manoeuvring?	❏ Yes ❏ No	If 'No', see paragraphs **550-567**, 608
Are they provided with horns, lights, reflectors, reversing lights and other safety features as necessary?	❏ Yes ❏ No	If 'No', see paragraphs **539**, 568-570, 608
Do they have seats, and restraints where necessary, that are safe and comfortable for the people using them?	❏ Yes ❏ No	If 'No', see paragraphs **541**, 1002-1008
Are there guards on dangerous parts of the vehicles, such as power take-offs, chain drives, exposed exhaust pipes etc?	❏ Yes ❏ No	If 'No', see paragraphs **542**, 750
Are drivers protected against bad weather conditions, or against an unpleasant working environment? Consider extremes of temperature, dirt, dust, fumes, and excessive noise and vibration.	❏ Yes ❏ No	If 'No', see paragraphs **646-647**
Is there a safe way of getting into and out of the driving position, and to or from any other parts that need to be reached?	❏ Yes ❏ No	If 'No', see paragraphs *53-54*, **498-522**
Does the driver need to be protected against injury in case the vehicle overturns? If there is a need, is this protection in place and strong enough?	❏ Yes ❏ No	If 'No', see paragraphs 549, **970-1008**

Vehicles *(continued)*

Does the driver need to be protected against being hit by falling objects? If there is a need, is this protection in place and strong enough?	❏ Yes ❏ No	If 'No', see paragraphs **549**, *1012*

5 *Check that the vehicles are maintained properly. For example:*

Do the drivers carry out basic safety checks before using vehicles?	❏ Yes ❏ No	If 'No', see paragraphs 452, **604-606**
Is there a regular preventive maintenance programme for each vehicle, carried out at set times or mileages?	❏ Yes ❏ No	If 'No', see paragraphs 346, 604, **607-608**
Where vehicles lift people or materials, there is a need for 'thorough examination'. Is this taking place?	❏ Yes ❏ No	If 'No', see paragraphs *611-617*

Drivers and other people

6 *Check that your selection and training procedures make sure that your drivers and other employees are able to work safely and responsibly. For example:*

Do you check the previous experience of your drivers and test them to make sure they are competent?	❏ Yes ❏ No	If 'No', see paragraphs 143-145, **642-648**
Do you provide training on how to do the job, and information about particular hazards, speed limits, the appropriate parking and loading areas etc?	❏ Yes ❏ No	If 'No', see paragraphs 144-145, *623-625* **642-665**
Do you have a planned programme of refresher training for drivers and other employees?	❏ Yes ❏ No	If 'No', see paragraphs **649-652**

7 *Check what your drivers and other employees actually do when carrying out their work activities. For example:*

Do your drivers drive with care? For example, do they use the correct routes, drive within the speed limit and follow any other site rules?	❏ Yes ❏ No	If 'No', see paragraphs *58*, ***128-153***, *620*
Do they park safely and in safe places?	❏ Yes ❏ No	If 'No', see paragraphs *58*, **409-427**
Are your employees working safely? Consider how they go about loading and unloading, securing loads, carrying out maintenance etc.	❏ Yes ❏ No	If 'No', see paragraphs *58*, ***128-153***
Are you sure that your drivers and other employees do not have to rush to complete their work on time?	❏ Yes ❏ No	If 'No', see paragraph **68**
Are you sure that there is no risk of accidents caused by tiredness as a result of working long hours?	❏ Yes ❏ No	If 'No', see paragraphs **68**, 463
Do managers and supervisors routinely challenge and investigate unsafe behaviour?	❏ Yes ❏ No	If 'No', see paragraphs **135-144**
Do managers and supervisors set a good example – for example, by following instructions to separate vehicles and pedestrians, and by wearing high-visibility clothing where needed?	❏ Yes ❏ No	If 'No', see paragraphs **135-136**

Drivers and other people *(continued)*

8 *Check, in consultation with your employees, that your level of management control and supervision is suitable. For example:*

Are your supervisors, drivers and other employees (including contractors and visiting drivers) aware of the site rules on using vehicles and traffic movement? Are they aware of their responsibilities to maintain a safe workplace and work safely?	❑ Yes	❑ No	If 'No', see paragraphs **126-134**, 170
Is everyone at the workplace supervised and held accountable for their responsibilities, and is a clear system of penalties enforced when employees, contractors etc fail to maintain standards?	❑ Yes	❑ No	If 'No', see paragraphs **135-144**, 154-171
Do you take adequate steps to assess the behaviour of pedestrians and drivers of site and visiting vehicles, to investigate any underlying reasons for unsafe behaviour, and to correct this?	❑ Yes	❑ No	If 'No', see paragraphs **135-144**, 621-665
Have you made certain people responsible for detecting, investigating and correcting unsafe behaviour?	❑ Yes	❑ No	If 'No', see paragraphs **132-136**

Vehicle activities

9 *Check that the need for reversing is kept to a minimum and, where reversing is necessary, that it is done safely and in safe areas. For example:*

Is there a one-way system on routes to reduce the need for reversing manoeuvres?	❑ Yes	❑ No	If 'No', see paragraphs **250-252**, *258*, *292*, 670
Are non-essential staff kept clear from areas where reversing is common?	❑ Yes	❑ No	If 'No', see paragraphs *258-263*, **371-392**, 674
Have you identified and marked 'reversing areas' to be clear to both drivers and pedestrians?	❑ Yes	❑ No	If 'No', see paragraph **673**
Are you sure that, where there is an unavoidable need to use a banksman (a signaller) to direct reversing vehicles, they are adequately trained and visible, and otherwise able to work safely?	❑ Yes	❑ No	If 'No', see paragraphs **683-697**
Are side-mounted and rear-view mirrors attached to the outside of the vehicles to provide the best all-round visibility?	❑ Yes	❑ No	If 'No', see paragraphs **550-557**
Have addiitional visibility aids, eg CCTV, been fitted to vehicles to eliminate or reduce blind spots during reversing?	❑ Yes	❑ No	If 'No', see paragraphs **558-564**
Do vehicles have reversing alarms?	❑ Yes	❑ No	If 'No', see paragraphs 565-570

10 *Check that drivers take care when parking their vehicles, including their own private cars, and that they park in safe places. For example:*

Do your drivers use the parking areas?	❑ Yes	❑ No	If 'No', see paragraphs 135-139, **413-416**
Do your drivers always put the brakes on for their vehicles and trailers and secure them before leaving them parked?	❑ Yes	❑ No	If 'No', see paragraphs **584-591**, 709-712, 719-720

Vehicle activities *(continued)*

11 *Check that loading and unloading is carried out safely. For example:*

Is loading and unloading carried out in an area away from passing traffic, pedestrians and others not involved in the work? Are you sure that people are not needlessly 'steadying' the load?	❑ Yes	❑ No	If 'No', see paragraphs 185-187, **748-751**, 799
Is there enough co-operation between the site occupier and duty holders who deliver or pick up goods? For example, are all the loads, the delivery vehicles, the vehicles that handle materials and the equipment compatible?	❑ Yes	❑ No	If 'No', see paragraphs **182-227**, 794-796
Is loading and unloading carried out using safe systems of work on ground that is flat, firm and free from potholes?	❑ Yes	❑ No	If 'No', see paragraph **748**
Are the vehicles braked and stabilised as appropriate, to prevent unsafe movement during loading and unloading?	❑ Yes	❑ No	If 'No', see paragraph **800**
Is loading and unloading carried out so that, as far as possible, the load is spread evenly to prevent the vehicle or trailer from becoming unstable?	❑ Yes	❑ No	If 'No', see paragraph **801**
Are checks made to make sure that loads are secured and arranged so that they cannot move about?	❑ Yes	❑ No	If 'No', see paragraphs **759-780**
Are checks made to make sure that vehicles are not loaded with more material than they can carry?	❑ Yes	❑ No	If 'No', see paragraphs **753-756**
Has the need for people to go on the load area of the vehicle been removed where possible?	❑ Yes	❑ No	If 'No', see paragraphs 806-809, **1009-1061**

12 *Check that tipping is carried out safely. For example:*

Do visiting drivers report to the site manager for any relevant instructions before tipping?	❑ Yes	❑ No	If 'No', see paragraphs 935, **939**
Are non-essential staff kept well clear of tipping areas?	❑ Yes	❑ No	If 'No', see paragraph **933**
Does tipping happen on ground that is level and stable, and at a place that is clear of overhead obstructions such as power lines, pipework etc.	❑ Yes	❑ No	If 'No', see paragraph **904**
Where sites are not level and stable, are the tipping faces safe for vehicles involved in tipping? For example, are they compacted and with no significant side slopes?	❑ Yes	❑ No	If 'No', see paragraphs **907-911**
Are suitably sized wheel stops provided where vehicles need to reverse before tipping?	❑ Yes	❑ No	If 'No', see paragraphs 679, **910-911**
Are tailgates secured open before tipping, and removed completely when necessary?	❑ Yes	❑ No	If 'No', see paragraphs **918-925**, 930-932
Do drivers check that their loads are evenly distributed across the vehicle before tipping?	❑ Yes	❑ No	If 'No', see paragraph **946**
Are the drivers experienced enough to anticipate loads sticking?	❑ Yes	❑ No	If 'No', see paragraphs **955-960**

Vehicle activities *(continued)*

Do drivers always make sure that the body is completely empty, and drive no more than a few metres forward to make sure the load is clear?	❏ Yes ❏ No	If 'No', see paragraphs **965-966**

13 Check that sheeting and unsheeting is carried out safely. For example:

Is sheeting and unsheeting carried out in a safe place, away from passing traffic and pedestrians and sheltered from strong winds and bad weather?	❏ Yes ❏ No	If 'No', see paragraphs 823, 828, **843**
Are the vehicles parked on level ground, with their parking brakes on and the ignition key removed?	❏ Yes ❏ No	If 'No', see paragraph **846**
Are gloves, safety boots and, where necessary, eye and head protection provided and used?	❏ Yes ❏ No	If 'No', see paragraph **878**
Is there room for using mechanical sheeting systems to avoid the need for manual sheeting?	❏ Yes ❏ No	If 'No', see paragraphs 832-837, **849-859**
Where manual sheeting is unavoidable, is there a system in place that avoids the need for a person to climb on the vehicle or load, for example by sheeting from the ground or by providing a platform from which loads can be sheeted?	❏ Yes ❏ No	If 'No', see paragraphs 498-522, 841-842, **868-887**

14 Check that coupling and uncoupling is carried out safely. For example:

Is the semi-trailer parking brake always applied before the hoses are disconnected, instead of using the emergency brakes to secure the trailer?	❏ Yes ❏ No	If 'No', see paragraphs **584-591**, 709-712, 719-720, 730-734
Do drivers check that the ground is able to support the semi-trailer and landing legs before uncoupling?	❏ Yes ❏ No	If 'No', see paragraphs **478-487**, 717, 732-734
Are landing legs always fully extended, properly padded and locked in place as necessary?	❏ Yes ❏ No	If 'No', see paragraphs 484-489, 581, **730-731**
Is the platform area behind the tractive unit kept clear, as clean as possible, and well lit, to help prevent falls?	❏ Yes ❏ No	If 'No', see paragraphs 725-726, **1057**
Do drivers know how to move any adjustable fairings to get behind their tractive unit easily, and are they doing so?	❏ Yes ❏ No	If 'No', see paragraphs **726**, *1010-1012*
Are the drivers experienced enough to know whether the fifth wheel is working properly?	❏ Yes ❏ No	If 'No', see paragraphs 631-632, **642-647**, 730
Are gloves and safety boots provided and used where necessary?	❏ Yes ❏ No	If 'No', see paragraph **729**
Are drivers wearing high-visibility clothing when they work around other moving vehicles?	❏ Yes ❏ No	If 'No', see paragraphs 235, 647, **729**

Appendix 2: Templates

You may reproduce these forms

Example of a workplace risk-assessment form

Risk assessment for:

Company name: _____

Location assessed: _____

Assessment carried out by:			**When the next review is due:**
Name: _____	Position: _____		_____
Signature: _____	Date: _____		

Step 1: **What are the hazards?** Photographs referenced here can support these entries.	**Step 2:** **Who is at risk, and how could they get hurt?**	**Step 3:** **How serious is the risk?**		
		Major, minor or acceptable?	What needs to be done to reduce the risk? Include anything already being done. Is it enough? There may be more than one thing for each risk. Record positive risk control, as well as action to be taken.	Decide on a deadline for anything that needs to be done. Make it as soon as possible. Major risks need to be dealt with quickly, but minor risks could be reduced very easily, and so the deadline might be sooner.

Example of a workplace risk-assessment form (continued)

Step 1: What are the hazards? Photographs referenced here can support	Step 2: Who is at risk, and how could they get hurt?	Step 3: How serious is the risk?		
		Major, minor or acceptable?	What needs to be done to reduce the risk?	Decide on a deadline.

Example of a driver training log

Employee's name: _____

Date started: _____

Date to review this summary sheet: _____

Road licence (attach a copy):

Driving licence?   ❑ Yes   ❑ No

Clean licence?   ❑ Yes   ❑ No

Specialist licence?   ❑ Yes   ❑ No

Type: _____

Training or qualifications (attach copies)

Course	Date achieved	Renewal date?	Checked?

Specific vehicles the employee is allowed to control:

1	6	
2	7	
3	8	
4	9	
5	10	All

Example of a driver and vehicle chart

Drivers	Vehicle 1	Vehicle 2	Vehicle 3	Vehicle 4	Vehicle 5
	Registration:	Registration:	Registration:	Registration:	Registration:

Glossary

ACOP Approved Code of Practice. An ACOP published by the Health and Safety Commission has a special legal status. It demonstrates behaviour that should be followed to meet regulatory provisions.

articulated used to identify a vehicle with a jointed body. Many types of vehicle can be articulated, such as lift trucks or construction site dumpers. The term is often used, however, to refer to articulated goods vehicle combinations. *See also* artic.

ATV all-terrain vehicle. ATVs are often 'quad bike' type, although a variety of designs are used in workplaces in Great Britain.

baffle an intermediate partial bulkhead that reduces the surge effect in a partially loaded tank. *See also* bulkhead.

baler a machine used to compress and bind materials (often agricultural or waste materials) for storage and shipment.

banksman a worker who guides a vehicle driver using signals.

barn doors a twin set of doors hinged on the outside.

bulk solid solid, particulate materials transported in bulk form, such as some grains, or mineral aggregate.

bulkhead a vertical partition in a load area. The bulkhead often describes the forward limit of the load area, and is often close to the rear of the cab.

cable lift a method for raising demountable containers onto transport vehicles, by means of a winch and cable.

camber the curvature of a road surface. The camber is measured as the height difference between one edge of the road and the centre.

CCTV closed circuit television.

close-coupled some types of vehicle are coupled with relatively little space between the tractive unit cab and the front of the trailer. 'Reefer' temperature controlled units are a good example, where the refrigeration equipment is often located in the usually empty area between the cab and trailer. *See* split coupling.

curtainsider a haulage vehicle with fabric sides on the load body, which are moved aside to allow access to the load down the sides of the vehicle.

competent person a competent person is somebody who has enough knowledge, experience and personal ability, and who has received enough training and information, to do a task safely and well. It may also mean a person chosen by the employer to carry out thorough examinations based on their level of knowledge of the equipment, problems and their causes, methods of testing and diagnosing faults.

demountable a load container that can be detached and removed from the carrying vehicle, such as a skip or a shipping container.

derate to lower the rated capacity. *See also* rated capacity.

desire lines the routes that pedestrian traffic choose to follow without guidance.

dipping lowering a device or measure into a tanker body, usually to measure quantity.

dock house a structure that extends out to meet the rear of a delivering goods vehicle and creates a seal between the vehicle load body and the warehouse bay.

dock leveller an adjustable ramp that covers the height difference between the vehicle and bay platforms.

dock shelter *See* dock house.

double dropside a vehicle on which both of the side walls of the load-carrying body are hinged and can be released for easier access onto the load bed.

double handling moving a load more than once.

drawbar a combination of a powered vehicle and a trailer. The trailer is attached to the vehicle by a hitch at the rear of the powered vehicle. Car trailers, rigid-truck trailers, caravans, and horseboxes are all examples of drawbar arrangements.

Driver and Vehicle Licensing Agency (DVLA) an Executive Agency of the Department for Transport.

dropside a hinged side wall of a vehicle load-carrying body, which can be released for easier access onto the load bed. Also used to refer to a vehicle with a dropside feature.

dunnage loosely packed bulky material such as boards, planks, blocks, or metal bracing, used in transportation and storage to support and secure loads to protect them from damage.

duty holder a duty holder is somebody who has a duty given to them by law. Every employer and worker is a duty holder in one way or another, because they have a duty to take reasonable care of themselves and other people.

fall arrest a harness system to reduce risks associated with work at height, which does not prevent a fall, but will make a fall less serious by stopping the worker from falling a long way.

fifth wheel the locking mechanism where the trailer connects to the tractive unit in an articulated goods-vehicle combination.

FOPS falling object protection system.

fork-lift truck a type of lift truck with forks extending forwards that are used to carry the load, which is usually on a pallet for this sort of vehicle.

fridge vehicle *see* temperature-controlled unit.

gantry normally a small platform with an overhead beam reaching over the area being accessed. A harness system is attached to the beam.

goalpost a three-sided structure put over a vehicle route to limit the width and height of vehicles that can continue.

grab refers to a wide variety of load-carrying equipment with moving parts that converge on or around the load. Often used to refer to the moving part of other machinery that converges on a load to secure it. Also frequently used as an alternative word for 'lorry loader', because this type of equipment often incorporates a grab. *See* lorry loader. Grabs are distinct from clamps, *see* clamp.

gross combination weight (GCW) the total weight of a fully equipped vehicle and any trailers, including cargo, equipment, driver and passengers and fuel.

ground loader a vehicle with a load body that can be entirely lowered to ground level to facilitate loading, avoiding the need for tail lifts, dock levellers and so on.

hammerhead a 'T' arrangement of two stubs opposite one another. *See* stub.

hardstanding places where vehicles and their trailers park up for any reason should be 'hardstanding'. They should be strong enough to safely support the weight of the vehicle, trailer and load as it rests on the surface (through the wheels and any outriggers or other stabilisers).

hazard a hazard means anything that can cause harm (for example, chemicals, electricity, working at height, machinery).

Hiab a brand of lorry loader. *See* lorry loader.

hooklift a type of demountable container, which is rolled onto and off the back of a carrying vehicle by a mechanical arm and hook arrangement fixed to the vehicle.

IBC intermediate bulk carrier.

inertia reel part of a fall-arrest system. An inertia reel acts much like a seatbelt, allowing free gentle movement but stopping anything sudden (like a fall).

just-in-time the ordering and delivery of products or materials so that they arrive 'just-in-time' for use, reducing the costs associated with storage.

jogging the practice of reversing then braking hard to free blocked material from a skip or tipped load body.

kingpin that part of the coupling mechanism in an articulated goods vehicle combination that is attached to the trailer, and locks into the throat of the 'fifth wheel' mechanism fixed to the tractive unit.

landing legs a supporting leg (often retractable) used to brace the front of a semi-trailer when it is uncoupled from the tractive unit of a vehicle combination. *See also* outrigger *and* padding.

load-spreading plates *see* padding *and* outrigger.

lorry loader a lorry-mounted crane, used to lift consignments onto or off the load bed.

mid-lift axle a retractable axle fitted to some larger vehicles, which can be lowered to provide extra support for heavy loads.

multi drop a delivery journey including unloading at several locations.

outrigger an extendable leg used to improve stability when a vehicle is stationary. *See also* load-spreading plates *and* padding.

padding material placed under the foot of an outrigger, landing leg or other support structure to spread the weight across a wider area and so reduce the pressure exerted on the ground. *See also* load-spreading plates *and* outrigger.

personal protective equipment (PPE) safety devices or safeguards worn or used by workers to protect themselves against one or more health and safety risks. Examples include high-visibility clothing, safety boots, gloves and safety harnesses.

pinch point in workplace transport safety route design, a narrowed part of a route put in place to encourage driving at low speeds.

power take off (PTO) a driveshaft, powered by the vehicle engine, which can be used to drive to an attachment or separate mechanism (such as the raising gear on a tipping vehicle).

PPE *see* personal protective equipment.

rear steer a vehicle with the pivoting wheel(s) positioned to the rear of the chassis, resulting in different turning characteristics than forward steer vehicles.

reasonably practicable the level of risk reduction that is usually expected of the duty holder. It implies that a risk has been thought about, and action to reduce it is reasonable compared to the chance of an accident happening and the consequences if it does.

reefer slang for temperature-controlled unit. *See* temperature-controlled unit.

rider-operated lift truck a lift truck that is capable of carrying an operator, including trucks operated from both seated and standing positions.

risk the chance that somebody will be harmed by a hazard (high or low) and how seriously they might be harmed (seriously or not).

risk assessment a careful examination of what, in your work, could harm people, so that you can weigh up whether you have taken enough precautions or should do more to prevent harm. You are legally required to assess the risks in your workplace.

roll-over protection system also called 'roll-over protective structure'. A structure intended to protect a vehicle operator and passengers if they would be likely to be crushed in the event of a vehicle overturn. An example might be a 'roll cage', or roll bars.

ROPS *see* roll-over protection system.

seat restraint a restraint intended to keep a vehicle operator or passenger in their seat.

segregation separation of two things, in particular pedestrians and vehicles.

semi-trailer the freight-carrying rear section of an articulated goods vehicle combination.

split coupling the practice of connecting the suzie hoses before coupling the tractive unit to the semi-trailer of an articulated goods vehicle combination, usually because the combination is 'close-coupled'. *See also* close coupled *and* suzie.

stub an area next to a road, intended to give drivers more room to manoeuvre.

suzie the air hoses and attachments that connect the semi-trailer systems to the tractive unit on an articulated lorry (UK standard). Other standards include the European 'palm' coupling and the North American 'glad-hand' standard.

swarf bin tipping-bin fork-lift truck attachment for bulk loads.

system of work a way of doing a task. A safe system of work has to be identified for every aspect of work that an organisation does, to make sure that people are able to work safely. It should be the result of a thorough risk assessment, which identifies what could harm people and how, so that these risks can be managed. The safe system should usually be written down so that workers can be instructed and their performance can be monitored.

tailgate the rear door of a load-carrying vehicle.

TCU *see* temperature-controlled unit.

temperature-controlled unit (TCU) an insulated container, often a semi-trailer, with a temperature-control mechanism for the benefit of loads that must be maintained at a certain temperature during transit.

three-point hold rule a person should keep at least three points of contact with the vehicle they are climbing (with their hands and feet), moving one limb at a time and testing the new hold before moving on.

tipping slang for unloading, as well as referring to vehicles with tipping load bodies, and the use of these vehicles.

traffic the movement of people and/or vehicles (often called *pedestrian traffic* or *vehicular traffic*).

tractive unit the powered unit of a vehicle and trailer combination.

tractor unit a widely used term for the powered unit of an articulated goods vehicle combination. *See also* tractive unit.

twist lock device for securing a shipping container for lifting or transit.

vehicle in this guidance, *vehicle* refers to all of the different vehicles found at the workplace, including mobile equipment.

Vehicle and Operator Services Agency (VOSA) VOSA is the merger of the Vehicle Inspectorate and the Traffic Area Network division of the Department for Transport. The aim of the agency is to contribute to the improvement of the road safety and environmental standards, and to the reduction of vehicle crime.

vibratory discharge system a system for discharging bulk powders from containers such as silos or tankers, which vibrates the powder, causing it to flow more freely.

wander lead a control device for a tail lift, allowing the operator to move away from the vehicle during the lifting operation.

workplace any location where a person is working. Public roads are public places and are covered by specific laws, so deciding when they are (or are not) workplaces can be complicated.

work-restraint system a fall-prevention system, which relies upon personal protective equipment (consisting of a harness and a lanyard), which is adjusted or set to a fixed length that physically prevents the person from getting to the place where they could fall. This system requires close supervision.

References and further information

References

1   *Reduce risks – cut costs: The real costs of accidents and ill health at work* Leaflet INDG355 HSE Books 2002 (single copy free or priced packs of 15 ISBN 0 7176 2337 8)

2   *Driving at work: Managing work-related road safety* Leaflet INDG382 HSE Books 2003 (single copy free or priced packs of 4 ISBN 0 7176 2740 3)

3   Redgrave A, Ford M *Redgrave's health and safety* Butterworths 2002 ISBN 0 406 95813 0

4   HSE Workplace transport website: www.hse.gov.uk/workplacetransport

5   *Successful health and safety management* HSG65 (Second edition) HSE Books 1997 ISBN 0 7176 1276 7

6   *Five steps to risk assessment* Leaflet INDG163(rev1) HSE Books 1998 (single copy free or priced packs of 10 ISBN 0 7176 1565 0)

7   *A guide to risk assessment requirements: Common provisions in health and safety law* Leaflet INDG218 HSE Books 1996 (single copy free or priced packs of 5 ISBN 0 7176 1211 2)

8   *Designing for Deliveries* Freight Transport Association 1983 ISBN 0 9029 9166 3 Available from The FTA, Hermes House, St John's Road, Tunbridge Wells, Kent TN4 9UZ. Tel +44 (0) 1892 526 171.

9   BS 7669-3:1994 V*ehicle restraint systems. Guide to the installation, inspection and repair of safety fences* British Standards Institution ISBN 0 580 22178 4

10 BS 6180:1999 *Barriers in and about buildings. Code of practice* British Standards Institution ISBN 0 580 33051 6

11 *Safe work in confined spaces. Confined Spaces Regulations 1997. Approved Code of Practice, Regulations and guidance* L101 HSE Books 1997 ISBN 0 7176 1405 0

12 Driving Standards Agency *The Highway Code* The Stationery Office 2004 ISBN 0 11 552449 5

13 *The safe use of vehicles on construction sites* HSG144 HSE Books 1998 ISBN 0 7176 1610 X

14 BS 873-1:1983 *Road traffic signs and internally illuminated bollards. Methods of test* British Standards Institution ISBN 0 580 130495

15 Department for Transport *Residential Roads and Footpaths: Layout Considerations* (Design Bulletin 32) The Stationery Office 1992 ISBN 0 11 752641 X

16 Chartered Institute of Building Services Engineers *Code for Lighting* Butterworth Heinemann 2002 ISBN 0 750 656379

17 *Lighting at work* HSG38 (Second edition) HSE Books 1997 ISBN 0 7176 1232 5

18 Department for Transport *The Safety of Loads on Vehicles: Code of Practice* The Stationery Office 2002 ISBN 0 11 552547 5

19 BS 4278: 1984 *Specification for eyebolts for lifting purposes* British Standards Institution ISBN 0 580 13801 1

20 BS 3551: 1962 *Specification for alloy steel shackles* British Standards Institution ISBN 0 580 35090 8

21 *Health and safety in motor vehicle repair* HSG67 HSE Books 1991 ISBN 0 7176 0483 7

22 *Hot work on vehicle wheels* Engineering Information Sheet EIS1 HSE Books 1992

23 Driver and Vehicle Licensing Agency *At A Glance* Available online at www.dvla.gov.uk

24 *Safety in working with lift trucks* HSG6 (Third edition) HSE Books 2000 ISBN 0 7176 1781 5

25 *Rider-operated lift trucks. Operator training. Approved Code of Practice and guidance* L117 HSE Books 1999 ISBN 0 7176 2455 2

26 BS 6736: 1986 *Code of practice for hand signalling for use in agricultural operations* British Standards Institution ISBN 0 580 15396 7

27 *Parking large goods vehicles safely: Guidance for drivers on coupling and uncoupling large goods vehicles (LGVs)* Leaflet INDG312 HSE Books 2000 (single copy free)

28 *Working safely near overhead power lines* Agriculture Information Sheet AIS8(rev2) HSE Books 2000

29 *Hiring and leasing out of plant: Application of PUWER 98, regulations 26 and 27* Information Sheet MISC156 HSE Books 1998

30 *Retrofitting of roll-over protective structures, restraining systems and their attachment points to mobile work equipment* Information Sheet MISC175 HSE Books 1999

31 *Fitting and use of restraining systems on lift trucks* Information Sheet MISC241 HSE Books 2000

32 *Safe use of all-terrain vehicles (ATVs) in agriculture and forestry* Agriculture Information Sheet AIS33 HSE Books 1999

33 *Safe use of work equipment. Provision and Use of Work Equipment Regulations 1998. Approved Code of Practice and guidance* L22 (Second edition) HSE Books 1998 ISBN 0 7176 1626 6

Relevant legislation

Health and Safety at Work etc Act 1974 Ch37 The Stationery Office 1974 ISBN 0 10 543774 3

Workplace (Health, Safety and Welfare) Regulations 1992 SI 1992/3004 The Stationery Office 1992 ISBN 0 11 025804 5

Reporting of Injuries, Diseases, and Dangerous Occurrences Regulations 1995 SI 1995/3163 The Stationery Office 1995 ISBN 0 11 053751 3

Health and Safety (Safety Signs and Signals) Regulations 1996 SI 1996/341 The Stationery Office 1996 ISBN 0 11 054093 X

Provision and Use of Work Equipment Regulations 1998 SI 1998/2306 The Stationery Office 1998 ISBN 0 1107 9599 7

Lifting Operations and Lifting Equipment Regulations 1998 SI 1998/2307 The Stationery Office 1998 ISBN 0 1107 9598 9

Management of Health and Safety at Work Regulations 1999 The Stationery Office 1999 ISBN 0 11 085625 2

Road Vehicles (Construction and Use) Regulations 1986 The Stationery Office 1986 ISBN 0 11 029069 0

While every effort has been made to ensure the accuracy of the references listed in this publication, their future availability cannot be guaranteed.

Useful organisations

British Industrial Truck Association www.bita.org.uk

British Safety Council www.britsafe.org

Consolidated Fork Truck Services
www.thoroughexamination.org

Fork Lift Truck Association www.fork-truck.org.uk

Freight Transport Association www.fta.org.uk

Health and Safety Laboratory www.hsl.gov.uk

Interpave (the Precast Concrete Paving and Kerb
Association)
www.paving.org.uk

Chartered Institute of Logistics and Transport
www.ciltuk.org.uk

BRAKE (the road safety charity) www.brake.org.uk

Road Haulage Association www.rha.net

Safety News www.safetynews.co.uk

Acknowledgments

Bentley Motors
Bombardier Transportation UK
British Sugar
Covers Timber Importers and Builders Merchants
Dr David J Edwards, Loughborough University
Dr Gary D Holt
Dr Will Murray, Interactive Driving Systems
Freight Transport Association
Istitut Nationale de Recherche et de Sécurité, France
Jewsons
London Borough of Barking and Dagenham
Marks & Spencer
NWF Group
Off-highway Plant and Equipment Research Centre (OPERC)
Paul Tolman
Plain English Campaign
Port of Felixstowe
Road Haulage Association
Road Haulage Liaison Committee
Transport and General Workers' Union
Wincanton Logistics for Somerfield

And the other individuals and organisations that have
contributed to or commented on this guidance.

Further information

HSE priced and free publications are available by mail order
from HSE Books, PO Box 1999, Sudbury, Suffolk CO10
2WA Tel: 01787 881165 Fax: 01787 313995 Website:
www.hsebooks.co.uk (HSE priced publications are also
available from bookshops and free leaflets can be
downloaded from HSE's website: www.hse.gov.uk.)

For information about health and safety ring HSE's Infoline
Tel: 0845 345 0055 Fax: 0845 408 9566 Textphone: 0845
408 9577 e-mail: hse.infoline@natbrit.com or write to HSE
Information Services, Caerphilly Business Park, Caerphilly
CF83 3GG.

British Standards are available from BSI Customer Services,
389 Chiswick High Road, London W4 4AL Tel: 020 8996
9001 Fax: 020 8996 7001 e-mail: cservices@bsi-global.com
Website: www.bsi-global.com

The Stationery Office publications are available from
The Stationery Office, PO Box 29, Norwich NR3 1GN
Tel: 0870 600 5522 Fax: 0870 600 5533
e-mail: customer.services@tso.co.uk Website:
www.tso.co.uk (They are also available from bookshops.)